Adventures In
NAKED
FAITH

Walking on Water in a World of Unbelief

ROSS TOOLEY

PUBLISHING
A Ministry of Youth With A Mission
P.O. Box 55787, Seattle, WA 98155

YWAM Publishing is the publishing ministry of Youth With A Mission. Youth With A Mission. (YWAM) is an international missionary organization of Christians from many denominations dedicated to presenting Jesus Christ to this generation. To this end, YWAM has focused its efforts in three main areas: 1) Training and equipping believers for their part in fulfilling the Great Commission (Matthew 28:19). 2) Personal evangelism. 3) Mercy ministry (medical and relief work).
For a free catalog of books and materials write or call:
YWAM Publishing
P.O. Box 55787, Seattle, WA 98155
(206)771-1153 or (800) 922-2143
e-mail address: 75701.2772 @ compuserve.com

Adventures in Naked Faith

Published by YWAM Publishing
P.O. Box 55787, Seattle, WA 98155, USA

ISBN 0-927545-90-X

Unless otherwise stated, all Scripture is taken from the HOLY BIBLE, NEW INTERNATIONAL VERSION. COPYRIGHT © 1973, 1978, 1984, International Bible Society. Used by permission of Zondervan Bible Publishers.

Scripture marked KJV are taken from the KING JAMES VERSION.

Printed in the United States of America.

To my dear wife

Margaret

with whom I have shared so many of these adventures

and to whom I owe so much

Other International Adventures

Foreword

Ross Tooley is a married man with four children who has been living without a salary for twenty-nine years. In those twenty-nine years, he can remember missing a meal only three times because he didn't have the money.

In his book, Ross shares ten principles of living by faith. Living by these principles is vital if you are to be a man or woman of God *whom God can trust*. The key issue of faith is not so much how we trust God but whether He can trust us. It is only as we live by the principles outlined in *Adventures in Naked Faith* that we become *faithful* people.

Ross Tooley bases his book on biblical principles and the character of God. He shares from his own experience, both his successes and his failures. As you live through his experiences with him, you will grow in your faith, and you will be challenged to base your decisions in life on the biblical principles that he outlines.

As I was reading this book, I began to think of young leaders whom I am mentoring and who I would want to read this book: I want the principles that Ross Tooley shares to become a foundation in these young leaders' walk with God. Some of them are facing some of the same challenges that Ross describes. In fact, every leader, every missionary, every man and woman of God will go through the same tests that Ross Tooley faced.

Why is that? It is because God sets up the circumstances in our life to make sure that our faith is tested. Tested faith is the only faith that is reliable. It is only in the crucible of life's difficulties that our faith grows strong—if we understand the nature of the test and discern how God wants us to respond.

Ross Tooley owns no credit cards, has run out of money in

uncountable countries around the world, has few or no assets, is not in debt, and has impacted nations for God. He has chosen to store up his treasures in heaven. I am challenged by Ross's example. I want to be a man of God, a man God can trust.

If you want to be a man or woman God can trust, this book is a must read. And after you read it, I know you will want to pass it on to young men and young women, to older folks who are at the crossroads of their life, to spiritual leaders, to ordinary people—all who should read this book. *Adventures in Naked Faith* is more than a great book—it is a way of life.

Floyd McClung
Director YWAM, Mission Village
Stonewall, Colorado, U.S.A.

November 1995

Contents

Acknowledgments

Elizabeth Sherrill, the well-known Christian author, looked worried as she lowered her voice to speak to me. "Ross, I'm concerned that when you leave Colorado you will be swamped with the other demands of your ministry and you'll never get to write this book!"

Less than two weeks before this conversation, God had provided finances (again at the last minute) for me to leave a sabbatical in New Zealand to attend a special writer's seminar. As Elizabeth and I spoke, I was conscious of the bus driver taking me to the Montrose airport to board. Quickly I reassured Elizabeth that until I returned to live in Hawaii—four months later—I would be able to spend much time on this project.

I arrived back in New Zealand that January of 1994 to find my wife Margaret very sick. Because Margaret took months to recover, we returned to Hawaii without my writing another word. Worse, I was as unsure as ever what format the book should take. The project was again on the back burner, as it had been for most of the ten years since Janice Cunningham Rogers had first enthusiastically suggested I start it. But I still believed I was to get writing—someday!

Sandi Tompkins, who attended that seminar in Colorado, invited me to join the writers' group she had formed in Kona, Hawaii. I happily agreed. At my first session, she turned to me and asked what I wanted to write about. I mentioned that I'd been thinking for a long time about a book on faith.

"Right," she said. "Let's have the outline next week!"

I was somewhat taken aback. I still wasn't sure how I should proceed. Dutifully, however, I went to work on the assignment.

At the next meeting of our writers' group, Sandi looked over an outline not too different from what has found its way into this volume.

"Okay," she said. "I'd like to see Chapter 1 next week."

Again I was taken aback. But I was off at last.

Sandi was not the only one used by God to motivate me. Other group members, including Yolanda Olsen, Joe Portale, Mary Vreeland, Roxanne Olsen, and Tanya Gunderson, were also instrumental in shaping my writing and offering me valuable ideas.

I am deeply grateful to Renee Taft Meloche for her timely admonishment early on to "just write an hour or so a day, Ross, five days a week." That advice was revolutionary. Who knows when this book would have surfaced otherwise!

Profound thanks to Scott Tompkins for the many hours he lovingly labored over this manuscript to place his editorial skills upon it. I marvel at his special skill in handling transitions that have shaped the text into a more logical presentation. My thanks go to Sandi for further polishing the manuscript when Scott had finished it.

Special thanks to my wife Margaret, who used her skillful line-editing talent on the manuscript. I am in awe at her ability to reduce five of my words to just one word, making the entire manuscript more readable. Her help was invaluable, since we had walked through many of these extraordinary adventures together.

I gratefully acknowledge the help from all these dear friends over the past eighteen months. Without this talented team, the book would not have emerged as it has.

Particular mention must be made of our Filipino friends whose lives enriched ours over the thirteen years we lived in their country. I grieve that it wasn't possible to mention all the friends with whom we shared so much and to whom we owe such a debt of gratitude. The adventures in this book deal with one particular subject— faith—and my editors kept me to it. In God's justice, however, I hope that I can someday tell some of the other stories of events not directly related to the subject of faith.

I extend deep gratitude also to the sometimes invisible army of people who have so generously given to Margaret and me over the past twenty-nine years. Some gave anonymously. Others, sacrificially. Many gave right at the crucial time, which in itself so often was the miracle. To those of you—family members, friends, acquaintances, and even strangers—who have supported us for many years, we offer you our heartfelt thanks.

Naturally, my deepest gratitude belongs to the Lord, whose gifts of guidance, protection, provision, and friends made all these stories possible. Thankfully, He is the same yesterday, today, and forever. We really can trust Him.

Ross Tooley
Kona, Hawaii

October 1995

Introduction
Land Mines on the Path of Faith

The roar of jet engines sent shivers of excitement through me as I approached the Rongotai airport in Wellington, New Zealand. The capital's new airport was buzzing with activity on its opening day. Newspaper articles about the air show had ignited my boyish interest, and I was looking forward to seeing everything.

Flying was a luxury far beyond our family's budget, but that didn't stop my youthful curiosity about airplanes. Family members had urged me to attend the air show, and two well-meaning adult Christians had given me an idea that made this more than a simple outing. They had encouraged me to go in faith and believe that someone would invite me to take my first ever plane ride. Although I was doubtful about this, I said I'd give it a try. I felt twinges of nervous excitement at the very thought of flying.

At the new airport, modern jets from the air forces of the United States, Great Britain, and New Zealand screamed overhead. Small propeller-driven planes executed breathtaking aerobatics to oohs and aahs of the crowd. Despite all this fun, I found myself oddly distracted. I was constantly pumping up my schoolboy faith. I walked around, looking for that someone who would invite me up in the air for a ride. But the joyride never came.

I went home feeling a failure in faith.

❧ ❧ ❧ ❧

I've learned a lot about faith since then. I believe that understanding God's principles about it can keep us from presumptions that cause disappointments like mine and even disasters like the one described by Yonggi Cho, pastor of the world's largest church in Seoul, South Korea, in his book *The Fourth Dimension*.

Dr. Cho recalls a time when Korean evangelist Sister Yun was conducting a week-long campaign on a Korean mountainside. Thousands of young people had flocked to her meetings, despite days of drenching rains. One day, a group of young people wanting to attend the meetings had congregated beside an overflowing river, their way to the revival meetings blocked. Seeing the muddy waters sweep past, most of the group became discouraged. But not three young women, who said to each other, "Let's believe God that we'll be able to walk on these waters!"

The women knelt to quote Scriptures and then prayed with great intensity. A little later, in full view of the rest of their group, they shouted and charged into the forbidding waters. Immediately they were swept away by the angry flood. Three days later their bodies were found in the open sea.[1]

This incident had serious repercussions, and some observers lost their faith. Many said the women had been told to boldly exercise their faith. Why, then, had God not supported the action of these three women?

What went wrong in these two incidents? Why didn't I get to fly, and why did the Korean women drown?

We had failed in at least one key area. We acted on our own, not at God's prompting. We ignored the fact that God specially spoke to Moses at the burning bush to lead the people of Israel out of Egypt (Ex. 3:10). It was not Moses' idea. We forgot that the walls of Jericho fell down because God specifically spoke to Joshua to march around that city seven times (Josh. 6:4-5). We failed to see that it was God who gave Elijah the idea of calling fire down from heaven (1 Kings 18:36).

In New Testament times, it was the unlikely person of Simon Peter who understood what faith is and isn't. In Matthew 14:24-26, the disciples were straining at the oars against a fierce night wind on the Sea of Galilee. Suddenly Jesus appeared walking on the water!

[1]. Adapted from *The Fourth Dimension* by Yonggi Cho (Logos International, Plainfield, N.J.), 1979.

True to his personality, Peter wanted to do that, too. Fortunately, his understanding of the Old Testament and his respect for the surly waters in the inky blackness restrained him. He first needed to be personally assured that this was God's will: "Lord, if that is you, tell me to come to you on the water" (Matt. 14:28).

Peter knew well the ferocious winds that swept down from the Galilean hills and whipped the lake into a frenzy. It would be foolish of him to attempt this without some word from God. He needed guidance.

The Lord gave Peter the invitation he was waiting for (Matt. 14:29). Clambering out of the boat with joy, Peter placed one foot, then both feet, on the surface of the lake. The waters held him! Peter was ecstatic!

Both the Korean young women and the apostle had the same goal in mind: to walk on the water. But the similarity stops there. Peter had the word of the Lord, while the young women didn't.

I carry a concern for many in the body of Christ who have launched out in faith but have done so without specific guidance from the Lord. The Korean women's story is obviously a tragic one, but so are other accounts of dedicated people who sold houses to do something for God and ended up in disillusionment and despair. The Christian landscape is strewn with the wreckage of those who have stepped out based on some enthusiastic emotion and their own good deed, without a word from God.

The purpose of this book is to explore the subject of faith by way of my personal experiences under the searchlight of Scripture.

My point is this: Whenever we step out in faith, we must have some go-ahead from God. Over the years I have learned that it is intolerable to try to have faith for something the Lord has not told me to do. To walk in faith can mean being buffeted on every side, with the temptation to give up often present. But it is a lot easier to do what I am attempting if I know that God has spoken to me.

Having a word from God means that He has given us a conviction that we should embark on a certain course of action for His glory. That word can come to us in a variety of ways:

(1) It can come as a response to prayer. The idea can grip us and stay in our hearts over a period of time until it's a settled persuasion. If the thought is really from God, it will not contradict the

written Word of God (Isa. 8:20), nor will it produce an uneasiness in our hearts. Peace (or lack of it) acts as an umpire (Col. 3:15). If we don't have that peace, it means that we should not go ahead, or at least that we should wait. We may also have to consider other dynamics, such as timing and having the right motivation.

(2) It can come as a bolt out of the blue. That is, we have an unshakable conviction of what we should do, right at the time we receive it. We call this kind of guidance a *rhema*, a time when God supernaturally shares a piece of His knowledge in an instant. Paul had a *rhema* when he knew a crippled man had faith to be healed in Acts 14:9-10. A *rhema*, however, will never contradict biblical principles, nor will it disturb inner peace.

(3) It can come through the written Word of God. Obeying the moral laws of God contained in the Scriptures demands faith. The book of Hebrews gives us a forceful example: "By faith Moses...chose to be mistreated along with the people of God rather than to enjoy the pleasures of sin for a short time" (Heb. 11:24-25). Moses knew it would be wrong to live on the fruits of evil and oppression.

Suppose we are battling with negative emotions, such as bitterness and envy, or a raging tide of impure thoughts. The Scriptures tell us that it is God's will that we should be holy (1 Thess. 4:31). We can therefore trust God for victory based on those Bible verses. Or suppose we're fascinated with the thought of marrying an unsaved person. The written Word of God quite clearly tell us that as Christians we can't (1 Cor. 7:39, 2 Cor. 6:14).

(4) It can come through the knowledge of God's character. What should we do when we need to make an urgent, critical decision and yet are unsure of God's will? This is where I have found the knowledge of God's character to be the most helpful. In such circumstances, I make a rational decision in the fear of God of what I think is the best for His kingdom, for my family, for the body of Christ, and for myself, and then I act accordingly.

Some would say that circumstances also play a part in guidance. I agree, but as you will see in the following chapters, they play a far less significant role than is commonly practiced. That's because I believe we are to go by the word of the Lord and then leave what happens to God. It can be dangerous to go by circumstances alone, believing that they reveal God's will; Satan can also open doors for us!

Had Moses followed circumstantial guidance, he would not have crossed through the Red Sea. He would have concluded that because the Red Sea was in the way, it was not God's will to proceed. We all know that Moses went by the word of the Lord. God then enabled the children of Israel to pass through the sea, which God had made into dry land (Ex. 14:21). I believe that our circumstances would change far more often if we were to follow Moses' example.

Perhaps you recall a time when you launched out in what you thought was faith but ended up disillusioned and hurt—perhaps even bitter. You may be hesitant to try anything in faith again. If this is true, you may want to ask yourself whether you really did have a word from the Lord. I certainly didn't when I "believed" for that joyride at the air show. I was acting on other people's good ideas, presuming this was God's will. I now see that because I moved in presumption, I can only blame myself for the resulting disappointment. That explanation may not satisfy everyone. Some may still believe they really did hear from God, even though their efforts came to nothing.

I hope that this book, which covers such issues as having right motives, persevering through trials, and waging spiritual warfare, will shed further light on why some dreams don't come to pass.

Once you have that word from the Lord, you can be confident in launching out in faith. But beware! Unbelief always seems to lurk at the gate.

A great scriptural example is the exodus of the children of Israel. God called the Israelites forth with a firm promise and liberated them from slavery through His awe-inspiring miracles. He also gave them a great leader, ample provisions, and protection from their enemies. But at key points of testing, the people quickly lapsed into unbelief and wandered aimlessly.

Everyone who follows God will be tested in this area. I did not know the problem I had with unbelief until I was faced with the challenge revealed in the following story. Even with a word from God, we need to root out unbelief or face bitter consequences.

CHAPTER ONE

Unbelief

Faith Enemy Number One

The weathered scaffolding crashed to the ground, setting off the clanging sounds of metal pipe, twisting and collapsing into a heap. Perched three stories above the newly constructed squash courts, I stopped to wipe perspiration from my eyes with the back of my rust-caked hands. I'd been tearing down scaffolding all morning and was happily visualizing my earnings piling up like the rusty pipe below. The money I earned on these special Saturday contracts was the ticket to my dream—a mission to the Philippines.

It was a gorgeous early summer's day, made all the more splendid by the view I had at treetop level. Wellington, at the southern tip of New Zealand's North Island, boasted a deep natural harbor ringed by hills of green and gold. Today in the sun our capital sparkled like a jewel. I knew I'd miss my home city, but inside I was singing. I was on my way to the mission field—at last!

As I calculated my wages, a thought popped into my head: *Give this money away.* I ignored it and immediately began to work even harder. But there it was again. It seemed so odd. I had already given a lot of money away to missions!

Since my conversion at age 15, I wanted to be a missionary more than anything else. In the four years since then, I had often pictured myself preaching the gospel in far-off lands. Now I had a real opportunity. Just weeks ago, Dal and Dorothy Walker, missionaries from my church, invited me to join their ministry in the Philippines for a few months. At first I rejected the idea. I felt I was called to South America. But in prayer several days later, a single thought gripped my mind: *Accept this invitation.* So I did.

I respected the Walkers and their family immensely and already felt a link to their ministry. Earlier, God had prompted me to give Dal a substantial gift to help him return to Manila. But now when I felt God call me to join them, I began to be concerned about my own need. The 28,000-ton ocean liner *M/V Oronsay* was due to sail for the Philippines in just two months, and I intended to be on it. That's why I had arranged with my boss to do this lucrative contract work on Saturdays.

Now this unwelcome thought was suggesting that I give these earnings away. This can't be right, I told myself. By afternoon I'd completely torn down the scaffolding and was sorting the pipes into neat stacks. As I stood to straighten my lanky frame and push away sweaty locks of fine blond hair, the thought persisted.

"Okay, Lord," I decided. "I'll give today's earnings away."

If God was speaking, who was I to say no? I might have to trust God for some of my needs I reasoned, but it wouldn't be all that much. After all, I still had two months to go.

All the next week, I worked hard with the construction crew. On Saturday, I was back alone on the jobsite, stripped to the waist, vigorously pounding nails to lay the wooden floor of the large building. Bathed in perspiration, I was content knowing these extra earnings would help cover my expenses for the Philippines.

Once again, I felt God's prompting to give my money away. Again, I resisted. But it was a case of obeying those inner urgings of the Holy Spirit or risk spoiling my walk with the Lord. God will supply, I thought, as if to convince myself. Sure, I knew He could, but why should He supply for me when I could earn it?

My plans to work harder and save more money collapsed when I fell and sprained my arm at a Christian retreat. Now I couldn't work at all. With departure just six weeks away, it was painfully obvious that I'd have to trust God to finance my five-month missionary endeavor. Fear began to rise up within me.

The phenomenon of people trusting God for their support was not new to me. I'd read biographies of Hudson Taylor, the famous missionary to China, and such other spiritual giants as George Müller and Rees Howell.[1] All were inspiring examples of this way of life. A number of full-time Christian workers I respected lived like this, and their rule of thumb was that you didn't advertise or hint about your needs. I had seen God provide a modern car for one of them, an English itinerant preacher named Arthur Wallis. Arthur hadn't advertised his needs, yet one of my roommates at Bible school had felt led to give him his new Austin 1100. I had been inspired at how this giving and receiving worked!

Because I believed that this way was right for me, too, I felt I couldn't suddenly turn to my church for help. Consequently, I said nothing. Everyone there assumed my job was bringing in more than enough.

Fear mounted within me as the days slipped by. Because I'd seen God supply even for me in the past, I'd always thought I had plenty of faith. When I began my Bible school training, I had no visible means of support. Yet unexpectedly, the mailman sometimes brought me letters stuffed with checks.

Why is this so different now?

As the day for paying my passage on the *M/V Oronsay* drew nearer, my levels of anxiety, unbelief, and even bitterness increased. I had financially helped others at God's call, but who now cared for me? I began to blame God for this injustice.

One day I pointed my old Ford Prefect toward the rugged seacoast near our family home in the Wellington suburb of Island Bay. I swung the car onto the road's grassy fringe. Even though I knew God had called me to go on this trip, in utter desperation I cried:

[1.] Please see note at end of the *Afterword* concerning biographies about these men.

"What is wrong with me God? Why can't I shake this black cloud of desperation?"

Above me, seagulls fighting against the stiff winds squawked back as if in mockery. The breakers pounding the craggy rocks nearby seemed to say it was no concern of theirs.

I reached for my Bible and read again those familiar verses from Isaiah 43:1-2: "Fear not, for I have redeemed you; I have summoned you by name; you are mine. When you pass through the waters, I will be with you; and when you pass through the rivers, they will not sweep you over. When you walk through the fire, you will not be burned."

My mind affirmed the message, but my emotions remained dead. I had been drowning in misery for weeks. Suddenly, I began shouting at the devil, rebuking him angrily for the depression I felt. The burden lifted momentarily, but soon that abysmal feeling of dejection clamped around me again like a thick, black blanket.

I had thrown myself into fasting, but after five days without food, my finances and my mood were as low as ever. What if God didn't provide until the last moment? Or worse, what if He didn't provide at all?

I still believed that telling someone about my needs was like breaking one of the Ten Commandments, so the only person I confided in was Mom. Because of our family circumstances, she couldn't offer a penny, nor did I expect her to. She suggested I seek spiritual advice from a godly woman named Joy Dawson who had counseled her just a few weeks before. I contacted the woman right away, but when we met, I told her about my debilitating fear and anxiety—not about my financial needs. But God quickly showed her that I was worrying about money for the trip.

This petite, middle-aged woman with dark hair and piercing eyes took her spiritual responsibilities seriously. She sat opposite me, intently taking in my every word. When I stopped talking, she began describing the sin of unbelief to me.

"You see," she said, "every sin has its root in unbelief and pride. You have allowed Satan a landing strip in your life from which he has been able to launch his attacks on you."

It made immediate sense.

She continued: "You need to see the sin of unbelief in your heart as God sees it. If you will seek for that revelation, God will give it to you. Only He can show you your heart, for in 2 Chronicles 6:30 we read that God alone knows the hearts of men."

I listened carefully and pondered her every word. But she was far from finished.

"I am happy to silently intercede now while you ask God to give you that revelation."

I agreed, and we both bowed our heads to start praying silently. At first I felt as dead as the rug beneath me. But then amazingly, I slowly felt myself coming under the power of the Holy Spirit's conviction. I saw my unbelief as ugly. From my inmost being I began to feel like weeping in contrition. But, ashamed to cry in front of a woman, I resisted the urge.

The conviction was so strong and real that I finally slipped off the couch onto my knees. Feeling embarrassed, I faced away from her and began crying tears of brokenness and deep sorrow for the state of my heart. I was very aware of a holy God and the evil way I had been thinking of Him.

"I'm sorry, Lord, that I have been mad at you and have judged you as being unfair," I sobbed.

I don't know how long I knelt there weeping in repentance, but I'll never forget the wonderful feeling of lightness and exaltation when the tide of grieving subsided. A freedom from fear. A happiness. Black clouds of anxiety had yielded to delight, and I began to laugh and laugh. I felt wonderfully clean and free. The unbelief was gone! I knew everything was all right now.

Then a thought slipped into my mind: Because I would pass through Australia en route to the Philippines, I told God that if all the money hadn't come in by the time I needed to leave New Zealand, I'd believe Him in Australia for the rest. Such was the deliverance I felt.

Financial breakthroughs soon followed. I sold my old Ford. Donations from completely unexpected sources brought in more money. I felt things were finally coming together. But on the day of my departure, I still needed sixteen New Zealand pounds—the equivalent of a week's pay as a construction worker. Four of the pounds were needed to pay for my Philippine visa. It was at this point that my faith began to quaver. As I threw my gear into the new travel bag the church had given me, I could feel the old feelings of injustice rising within me.

Why haven't I received all my money? I queried inwardly as I paced from room to room looking for last minute things to pack. I allowed these feeling to rage on for quite a while. But finally I determined, more by will than by emotions, that if I had to trust God to provide those last sixteen pounds on the way, so be it. I was off.

My dad was on duty that afternoon at the hospital where he worked as a male nurse, and so Mom came with me to the train station. I was delighted to see that some of the church's young people's group had come to say goodbye. Just before the departure whistle blew, Gary, our youth leader, handed me an envelope. Once the train got rolling, I tore open the envelope. Inside was sixteen pounds. Thank you, Lord! What a wonderful provision!

Gary could not have known how perfectly timed—and needed—his gift was. I began thinking of all that I had gone through over the past several months. I felt ashamed of all the unbelief I had indulged in. I had learned a hard lesson in faith; but thankfully, I had learned it, and now this test was over.

I settled back to catch a last glimpse of Wellington's spectacular harbor shimmering in the late afternoon summer sun. My mind relaxed, and a warm feeling of contentment and excitement washed over me. As the train was about to plunge into the dark tunnels that would carry me through the hills away from my hometown, I remembered something. And froze.

I had forgotten to repay my father the five pounds I owed him. If I gave him the money, I wouldn't have enough to pay the Philippine visa fee after all!

Couldn't I just use that money, I thought, *and pay Dad back later?* I knew that my father wouldn't mind. But that wasn't the issue. I was on a pilgrimage of faith.

As the train jerked and swayed inside that long black tunnel, so did the arguments both for and against either course of action. The debate raged inside me most of the fourteen-hour journey to Auckland, New Zealand's largest city. I finally determined to pay

Dad back. I couldn't imagine George Müller or any of my other spiritual heroes taking the easy way out.

The next morning the train arrived at the outskirts of Auckland, a city built on the isthmus where the Pacific Ocean and the Tasman Sea almost meet. As the train hugged the coast on its approach to downtown, I could see yachts dotting the picturesque harbor. I would be on those very seas that night. But first I needed to find a post office.

An hour after arriving, I pushed an envelope addressed to my father through the brass mail slot at Auckland's chief post office. As I plodded down the steps, my heart was in my mouth.

I was now down to my last grubby bank note, not enough to pay for my visa. But God would supply somehow. Six hours later I walked up to the gangplank of the huge white ocean liner. Once on board the *Oronsay*, I had an unearthly feeling. I was leaving my country for the first time and doing it short of the money I needed, just as I'd told God I would.

Then to my great surprise, the steward escorted me to my lodgings—a first-class, single-berthed cabin! He explained that I could use this only until Sydney, but even so, I laughed at the irony. With only a pittance in my wallet, I lived in luxury and dined sumptuously during the trans-Tasman crossing.

Three days later we sailed into Sydney's Port Jackson and docked close to the harbor bridge. As I peered through the porthole in my cabin, I could see the stunning white curves of Sydney's opera house glistening in the morning sun. Once we'd docked and cleared immigration and customs, I quickly discovered that the Philippine embassy would close for the weekend the following day, Friday, at 5 p.m. I would need four pounds by then or have to leave the ship before it sailed on Sunday at noon.

After buying stamps, I was down to just five cents, which I used to take the ferry to a prayer meeting that night on Sydney's North Shore. As the ferry glided into the harbor, I could see that even though Sydney's homes and buildings were similar to those in New Zealand, I felt like a stranger.

My funds were now completely depleted. I fully expected God to supply the money for my visa at the service. I was even given the opportunity to preach and was asked to share about my trip to the Philippines. But no money came in. Had I not been driven over the harbor bridge back to the ship, I might have been stranded.

I spent a lot of time praying the next day. I still needed four pounds for a visa, and the deadline was closing in. At about 4:30 p.m. I walked, half urgently, half hesitantly, up George Street to the Philippines consulate to do the only thing I felt impressed to do: explain that I didn't have the necessary four pounds, and see what would happen.

Once inside, I told the Australian woman behind the counter that I was on the *M/V Oronsay* and that I wanted a four-month visa.

"But there is a problem," I started, feeling very self-conscious. "I've been expecting some money, but it has not arrived."

I was being quite truthful. I just didn't tell her I had been expecting it from God.

"Why don't you check with the purser's office on board the ship?" she said.

"I have done that several times," I replied. It was embarrassing to apply for a stay of four months when I didn't even have the money for the visa fee! Finally, she said, "Please wait here. I will have to talk to the consul about this."

Without the visa I would be stranded in Australia without even coins to make a phone call.

"O Lord," I prayed under my breath, "Everything hinges on this. Let them grant me this visa somehow!"

I was praying silently with my eyes open looking in the direction of the consul's office. I kept praying hard for the conversation going on behind the door. Finally, the door swung open and out strode the woman.

"The visa that would have cost you four pounds in New Zealand," she started, "is actually free of charge here in Australia. Could you take a seat over there while we stamp your passport?"

Ten minutes later, I still didn't have a penny to my name as I weaved through the crowded pedestrian traffic to return to the ship. But with a spring in my step and the visa stamped on my passport, I thought I must be the happiest man in Sydney!

Dealing with Unbelief

Many times over the years, the truths I learned on that counselor's floor as a 19-year-old have helped me through many a crisis. I've often needed to remember that experience of spiritual surgery to keep me from lapsing into unbelief which I am prone to do. I have to resist it because unbelief attributes to God characteristics that don't belong to Him: that He is unfair, that He will fail us, that He doesn't care. But God is just; God never fails; God does care.

When the Bible says, "without faith, it is impossible to please God" (Heb. 11:6), it means just that. Unless we believe in God's character and act accordingly, we can only anticipate failure. God wants us to expect Him to be loving and kind. Consider Psalm 147:11: "the Lord delights in those...who put their hope in his unfailing love."

In my view, unbelief was the sin that grieved Jesus the most when He was on earth. Luke 8:22-25 tells of Jesus in the boat with His disciples after having given the command to cross the Sea of Galilee. While He was asleep, a violent storm developed, and the wind-swept waves began filling the boat. Terrified, the disciples woke Jesus. They were desperate, believing they were going to drown. Jesus merely stood up and rebuked the storm, and all was calm.

Someone reading this story for the first time could be mystified with Jesus' reprimanding question: "Where is your faith?" Hadn't the disciples exercised it already? Hadn't they acknowledged His power and deity by calling on Him to do something? Why the rebuke? I believe Jesus was disappointed that they didn't have faith in the character of God to believe He'd answer *their* prayers.

It is a sin to not have faith in God's benevolent attributes and to wallow in fear, despondency, and self-pity. We must confess and forsake that sin. To walk by faith requires our dealing decisively and drastically with unbelief whenever it raises its ugly head.

God has purposed that we demonstrate that we are his sons and daughters. He has given all of His children—not just pastors, teachers, and evangelists—authority to minister in His name. He has an obsession for all to hear His gospel (1 Tim. 2:4), and we have been given the privilege of being His ambassadors.

We come up with all kinds of excuses why we can't be used by God. We think we are too young—or too old. Perhaps we're like Moses and think we're not a good enough speaker or not educated enough. Whatever the excuse, we must remember that it's not our abilities we're to trust in, it's our faith in God's loving and steadfast character.

God soon showed my Filipino friends and me that He will use all of us for His glory if we're willing to take even small steps of faith.

Chapter Two

God Wants to Use Us All

My first two months in the Philippines fully immersed me into missionary life. Within two weeks of my arrival in Manila, I was headed for the southern Philippine island of Mindanao, where the Walkers were about to hold evangelistic meetings in two cities. Everything in these steamy, bustling cities was so different from the quiet countryside where I had grown up in New Zealand. I walked the streets, soaking up the unusual sights, smells, and sounds of this new land and its culture. From the first day, I loved it.

I also drank in the rich teaching of an Australian pastor who assisted Dal Walker in the nightly preaching under the crusade tent. During morning meetings the pastor taught us to embrace our identity as sons and daughters of the living God.

"God wants all to be saved," he preached persuasively from 1 Timothy 2:4. "Jesus died and rose again to make this possible. We should live with that in mind and step out and do exploits in faith. If you are a Christian, you should really believe God for great things!"

Inspired by his teaching, my faith soared. Despite my youth, I was given opportunities to preach in local churches and at the city jail, and each opportunity to witness for Christ gave me faith to believe for bigger things. I marveled at how God was using me, a strange young foreigner, to share His good news with the Filipino people. On the ship sailing back to Manila, God gave me further evidence that He was launching me into thrilling new adventures in faith.

Three Filipinos and I were asked to take the huge crusade tent, some 16mm films, and other campaign equipment back to Manila. As we arrived at the dock in Davao (Dah-VOW), cranes creaked under the weight of the freight being loaded into the ship's holds. Passengers laden with baggage soon streamed towards the gangways. Passing among them were vendors loudly hawking food, drinks, and cigarettes. We unloaded the tent on the dock and struggled aboard with the other equipment and baggage.

Following my companions, I came to a covered open deck where long lines of stretcher-like cots rested butted up against each other. This was to be our dorm during the voyage, which in 1966, took five days and six nights. Many passengers who had arrived before us were lying on their cots with bundles of cargo nearby. I tried to stretch out on my cot, which was easily six inches too short for my six-foot-two frame. When I finally got reasonably comfortable, I surveyed the curious scene around me. Occasionally, I heard a rooster crow from a cage made out of a cardboard box. Below us near the ship's holds, pigs grunted while water buffaloes munched contently. What a difference compared to the *M/V Oronsay*!

On the Davao pier, one of the ship's crewmen had viewed our cans of 16mm films with great interest. During the long voyages in those days, Philippine ships routinely showed films on deck at night, projecting them onto a large piece of whitewashed plywood. Tired of seeing the same films over and over, this crew member was hopeful we might have something different to present. He asked whether they could screen one of our films. Remembering the exhortations of the Australian pastor, I was excited at this opportunity to reach people for Christ!

"Of course," I replied.

Once at sea, the ship creaked under its weight of passengers, freight, and livestock, which included twenty-five water buffaloes and two hundred fifty pigs. With just a small cot to live on for five days, many of the passengers slept to escape boredom.

A day or two out of Davao, I suggested to my companions that we distribute gospel tracts to the hundreds and hundreds of passengers on board. People eagerly reached out to receive something to read, and they attentively listened as we testified to Christ. After all, in the cramped conditions they couldn't go far!

After our initial tract distribution, I witnessed by myself through the different passenger sections. I even visited the crew's quarters and the captain's bridge. I prayed with the ship's doctor to receive Christ and began to see a change in him over the next few days. I was fired up by the concept that we were sons of the living God who wanted none to be lost (Matt. 18:14).

By the final night of the trip, I was disappointed that none of our films had been screened. Was it because I had been witnessing so much that they just knew our films would be too religious? I didn't know.

If I don't do something tonight, I reasoned, *this golden opportunity will be lost forever.* I approached one of the crew members and asked what he could do.

"Okay!" he said in Filipino English, which often places a drawn-out stress on the last word of each sentence. "We will show your film tonight!"

Happily I returned to my cot. But sometime later, I heard a noise coming from the deck below. I sat bolt upright at what seemed like a movie soundtrack. How could that be? I hadn't even given them the film yet! I scurried through the ship to the projection area, where my heart sank. There on the screen was the unmistakable image of *Tom Sawyer!* I found the projectionist and bent down to his height.

"I thought you were going to show our film...."

"It's okay!" he shouted over the clatter of the projector. "We will just view your film at the end of this one."

My heart sank further. *Tom Sawyer* was three reels long! Perhaps he read the disappointment on my face, for he continued to speak right into my ear.

"Or, if you like, we can show it after the first reel of this film!"

"Okay," I said, my spirits lifting, "let's do it after the first reel of *Tom Sawyer!*"

But I also wanted to be able to preach. This was in keeping with the revelation I had received that God wanted Christians to do exploits in faith. But how does a just-turned 20-year-old invite himself to preach the gospel openly on a foreign ship sailing the high seas?

Earlier, I'd had an idea. The campaign film I'd chosen contained a powerful message of deliverance from demon power. It was the true story of a prostitute, an inmate of a Manila jail. Despite the best efforts of doctors and psychologists, this young woman had continued under the powerful influence of demonic forces. The attacks were so vicious that her case had made news headlines. A Manila radio station even carried these attacks live. No Christians had come forward to help until God spoke to an American missionary-evangelist to pray for the young tortured woman.

"Our film is a bit unusual," I started, still speaking loudly above the soundtrack of *Tom Sawyer*. "I'll need to be able to explain it afterwards. Would you allow me to stand on the ship's hold with a microphone and talk about it?"

To my delight, he agreed. I hurried back to my cot and brought my two technician Filipino companions up to date. Not stopping to catch my breath, I asked if they could arrange the sound. They nodded.

"And, oh yes, José, could you interpret for me?"

To my knowledge, the 22-year-old had never interpreted before, but José agreed. Did he sense that God wanted to use him, too, during this outstanding opportunity?

When our movie hit the makeshift screen, the audience quickly identified with the young Filipina's story of hardship and deprivation. Most Filipinos are aware of the evil spiritual realm, and our film kept them riveted to the screen. As the movie built to a climax, the forces of righteousness were locked in deadly combat with evil. The demons would leave the prostitute, but then would return. It took prayer and fasting and long sessions over a two-day period before she was finally delivered in that jail, right in front of the eyes of the watching media. What a victory for the kingdom of righteousness!

After the film, the atmosphere was heavy with query and expectation as José and I, microphones in hand, climbed up onto the hold. Our youthfulness did not seem to matter a bit. About eighty people took in every word as we explained the meaning of the film. I then preached about our need to be born again and to turn from everything we know is wrong. José interpreted my words without faltering. When I asked for a response, about forty hands reached towards the stars, which seemed to twinkle back at us with excitement.

I noticed the projectionist putting away his equipment despite the fact that two more reels of *Tom Sawyer* were scheduled. Perhaps the projectionist didn't think it was appropriate to show the rest of the movie. I had to agree.

I hadn't yet learned that in the Philippines it is quite easy to get people to respond to a gospel message. Many Filipinos describe themselves as *Ninas Cogan*, meaning they get excited easily about something different but soon lose interest. That understanding would come in time. Even so, as I lay on my cot with barely a peso in my pocket, nothing could take away the joy of seeing God open a door of opportunity in response to our firm belief that Jesus wanted people to hear His good news.

As the heaving rhythm of that creaking ship lulled me off to sleep on that open deck, I felt disappointed knowing that it was late at night and we would be docking in Manila at dawn. Everything within me wanted to comb the ship and find those who had raised their hands to follow Christ.

🕮 🕮 🕮 🕮

Soon after our eventful trip back from Davao I was invited on other ministry trips to the provinces south of Manila. On one such outreach with José and the singing Barruel brothers, we desperately needed a miracle. Night after night our open-air meetings in the town plaza were washed out by torrential rain. We would find ourselves stuck in the church building, where the sound of the heavy rain on the tin roof would make normal conversation impossible. Then the next day the sun would shine from a blue sky as if to mock us. I finally approached the American missionary in charge of the meetings with whom I had established a friendly rapport.

"I can't see it's God's will that people miss hearing His message of salvation because of all this rain. Shouldn't we pray for a break in the weather tonight?"

He said nothing, but nodded thoughtfully.

That morning in the team meeting, we stormed the heavens in prayer. Not a drop of rain had fallen when we arrived at the plaza that evening. That in itself was progress. As we ended the rainless service, including the prayer time for those seeking salvation and healing, I was ecstatic.

After the service, we loaded up our equipment, piled into our Volkswagen van, and made our way home through the dark and pothole-ridden streets. We'd just entered the church building when, like a mighty burst of machine-gun fire, torrential rain struck the tin roof. I stood for a moment in awe. God had heard our little team's prayers and kept back the rain until we had preached His word!

God wants to use you!

Many of us feel so inadequate when it comes to serving God. But part of operating in faith, I believe, is to consider things from God's perspective. Jesus died and rose again so that the Kingdom of God could advance. Is it any glory to Him if we continually meditate on our disappointments in life and forget His eternal purposes?

Jesus said, "I will do whatever you ask *in my name*, so that the Son may bring glory to the Father" [emphasis added] (John 14:13).

In my view, to pray in Jesus' name does not mean just adding those three words at the end of a prayer. It means that Jesus would receive the benefit and glory if the petition were granted. God's eternal purpose is tied up with the cross, and He wants the message of "repentance toward God, and faith toward our Lord Jesus Christ" (Acts 20:21, KJV) to be scattered far and wide. That is why "this gospel of the kingdom will be preached in the whole world..., then the end will come" (Matt. 24:14).

True, we must be sensitive to any guidance by the Holy Spirit. Acts 16:7 says, "...they tried to enter Bithynia, but the Spirit of Jesus would not allow them to." This was probably a conviction in the heart of the apostles brought about by lack of peace. Obviously, the more sensitive to the leading of the Lord we are, the more effective we will be.

Some might object to our praying against the rain in the preceding anecdote. They may feel that since God controls the weather, it's useless to interfere with His will. But we had a real conviction that we *should* pray.

At least two places in Scriptures give us reason to believe someone other than God has the ability to dispatch rain and storms. In Job, chapter one, God gave Satan permission to harass Job and his family. One of the first things the devil did with that permission was to hurl a mighty wind against Job's son's house. The house collapsed, causing great loss of life (Job 1:12-19).

In Luke 8:24, the disciples were swamped in a storm on the Sea of Galilee while Jesus lay asleep at the back of the boat. Convinced they were all going to drown, the disciples awoke the Lord, who immediately "rebuked the wind and raging waters." The word *rebuked* is the same word Jesus used for casting out demons. Now, if Jesus believed the storm came from God, why did He address it as He would an evil spirit?

Our team wasn't trying to impress anyone with our faith when we prayed for God to hold back the rain. We simply asked Him for the opportunity to declare His word. As sons and daughters of God, we can all ask our Father for opportunities to advance His kingdom. He wants us to trust Him for such things.

One of the joys of my time in the Philippines in the years to come was seeing Filipino friends enter a personal revelation of their sonship. Although many were reluctant at first to launch out, once they understood who they were in God, they realized that our Father is no respecter of persons. God loves all His children and wants to do great things in and through their lives.

The good news is the gospel of God's grace. Yet the Scriptures also say a lot about works, not that we are to work for *salvation, but rather we are to work* from *it. The Bible declares that we are created in Christ Jesus to do good works, which God prepared in advance for us to do (Eph. 2:10). To find out what we are to do is part of our walk in faith. I learned another valuable point about faith when God graciously guided our ministry team to do the very thing that was on His heart.*

CHAPTER THREE

Faith Without Works Is Dead

By now, it was abundantly clear to me that God was guiding my walk of faith as a missionary. When I returned to New Zealand in 1966, He opened up opportunities for me to preach throughout the country—even though I was only 20 years of age. These opportunities always followed steps of faith that God showed me to take, but I was still amazed with each opportunity. God continued to supply my needs without my asking anyone for help. Despite these wonderful openings in my home country, I still longed to be working in the mission field, sharing my life and ministry with a partner at my side.

In 1967, God led me into two relationships that would dramatically influence the course of my life. The first was Loren Cunningham, the visionary founder of Youth With A Mission (YWAM). The second was with my then future wife.

I met Loren Cunningham at a New Year's convention, where he was introducing his young program to New Zealand. I immediately took a liking to this 31-year-old Californian and his friendly ways.

One evening, I told Loren of my interest in South America. He proceeded to draw a map of the continent and began to outline his vision for that part of the world.

"We're about to send a pilot team into Latin America, and there is one place left in our van. It's about to leave shortly, but I'll call Los Angeles and save a place if you feel that seat is for you."

My pulse quickened and I sat up straight in my chair. I could hardly believe my ears! Since high school days I'd wanted to be a missionary to South America, but nothing had opened up despite all my efforts. This sounded like just the opportunity!

Despite all my praying over the next few days, I received no guidance from the Lord. I had to pass on the trip, and I heard later that it had been called off. My teenage dream of being a missionary to South America was never fulfilled, but a couple of weeks later I joined YWAM as its first non-North American member and only its eleventh full-time worker in the world. Six weeks later, I ventured out on my first YWAM outreach with a team to the South Pacific.

On my return to New Zealand I started recruiting workers for our next target—the South Pacific kingdom of Tonga. While on my recruiting circuit, I received a last-minute invitation to speak at a church in Wellington. As I gave my best call-to-missions pitch, a dark-haired young woman in the back pew drew my attention for a moment. Something about her manner made me feel she really knew God. Just that. Since I had no intention of pursuing her, it took a series of little miracles over the next twelve hours to bring me and Margaret Keys together. When God did bring us together, something wonderful happened. Margaret captured my heart. At the time we met, my departure for a two-month outreach to Tonga was just ten days away. I knew I had to work quickly.

I arranged to see Margaret several times before I left, and we agreed to write. Through those letters and her dedicated praying for that outreach, our friendship developed into love. Over the next two years, we saw each other every time I visited my hometown of Wellington. We were married in the nearby city of Lower Hutt on April 19, 1969.

Margaret and I spent the first eight months of our marriage leading the work of YWAM in New Zealand. At year's end, together with my brother Max, we took thirty-five young New Zealanders on an outreach to Indonesia. Margaret and I stayed on for an additional six months to travel in Asia. I took that opportunity to introduce my bride to the Philippines. My fond thoughts had often returned to my adopted home, and I was preparing to launch a new outreach there. The plan was to travel throughout Asia for fourteen months, starting and finishing in the Philippines. During our trip, our YWAM team would be witnessing and training others in evangelism.

We recruited a team of eleven, which we called the Asia Circle Team, and hoped that many of them would remain doing the work of the Lord long-term. At the end of this fruitful year of ministry in 1971, God directed us back to Davao in the Philippines. I felt strangely attached to this southern port city, situated between the emerald waters of the Davao Gulf and the majestic cone-shaped Mount Apo. When I smelled the sweet pungence of drying coconuts hanging in the air, I knew I had arrived.

Since most of the members of our Asia Circle Team had moved on, God brought together another group of dedicated workers. Still with us after a year was Mike Shelling, a quiet, dependable young Australian who wore dark-rimmed glasses. Mike stood just five-foot four, but this faithful brother was a giant in his dedication to God. Among the new recruits was Graeme Jones, a redheaded New Zealander with a delightful, wry wit. We didn't know it then, but these two cheerful young men would become dear friends and coworkers for many years to come.

Our new eight-member team decided to travel for three months through the island of Mindanao teaching about personal evangelism, much as we'd been doing on the Asian mainland over the past year. We had planned to spend two weeks with each church, teaching church members by taking them on a practical house-to-house evangelism experience.

The missionary in charge of our schedule approached us with another prospect. Could our team spend the whole three months with a struggling church in Davao whose pastor had just resigned? This would be a radical change from anything Margaret and I had ever done in our five years with YWAM. As we prayed as a team for direction, we felt God confirm that we should accept this short-term offer. This confirmation gave us confidence to launch out in faith. Although we knew that the Lord "prepared in advance [the good works] for us to do so" (Eph. 2:10), we wondered how to proceed.

Our first step was to find a place to live. The church was housed in a two-story commercial building in an old part of town. By putting up partitions in the large upstairs room, we created three "bedrooms," one for the women, one for the men, and one for Margaret and me. Although the plywood partitions did not reach the ceiling and were certainly not soundproof, we considered this makeshift suite of rooms to be home.

Our more serious concern was how to build up the church. This was no ordinary congregation. It consisted mainly of students from a Bible school with few unsaved friends or family members nearby. As a result, we had no natural network from which to draw in new members. To make matters worse, because everyone passing by could see into the old storefront building, it was difficult to invite our street contacts to church, because they felt intimidated and self-conscious.

Our first strategy came through a revelation to Margaret during a team meeting.

"I was impressed with a Scripture during this morning's Bible reading," she started in her sweet, clear voice. "It's found in Isaiah 62:6-7. It reads, 'You who call on the LORD, give yourselves no rest, and give him no rest till he establishes Jerusalem.'"

By now, we were aware that the church needed a spiritual breakthrough with sinners getting converted. We knew it was easy to get people to lift their hands to the Lord in a gospel meeting in the Philippines, but quite a different thing to see them become consistent church-going disciples.

Inspired by the verses in Isaiah, we decided to do something bold: the eight of us maintained an around-the-clock prayer vigil; each of us prayed for an hour, three times a day. We began to intercede for the nation facing growing anarchy and chaos, for the city God had called us to, for our ministry to the church, and for the contacts we made witnessing in the streets.

This prayer vigil complemented our other activities as we continued to witness and invite people to attend services. Newcomers continued to appear at the open double doors of the church but remained reluctant to step inside. They stood anchored to the sidewalk listening intently but would venture no farther.

One night I came up with another strategy. *If they aren't going to take a seat inside,* I mused, *they may as well feel part of the service while on the footpath!*

We lugged wooden benches onto the sidewalk. One of the first to make use of them was Rey Yap, a doctor's son who lived a block away. Although Rey did not give his life to Christ that night, he befriended us and even paved the way for us to speak in many classrooms at his school, Holy Cross College of Davao, just around the corner.

In each class we always found activist students interested in overthrowing the government. To grasp their attention, I deliberately preached about the revolution of Jesus Christ: that internal spiritual upheaval within a non-Christian that turns us from a life of selfishness. I knew I was speaking directly to those advocating a violent uprising with the use of guns and bombs. The atmosphere on college campuses at that time was so highly charged that I half expected someone to fire a shot at me while I spoke in class or place a bomb under the church building while we slept. Oddly, we sensed no fear. Was it all the praying that caused us to feel this way?

We continued to pray. With only eight on the team, each person's one-hour vigil came round quickly. No matter what the team was doing, we excused the person whose turn it was to intercede. We prayed for everything we could think of. Sometimes it was easy. Mostly it was hard work. But after a few weeks, things began to happen.

The first to make a move was a petite college student named Helen, who broke her heart before the Lord at the altar call one Sunday. After Helen's conversation, one of our team members, Lois, met with Helen most afternoons to pray, study the Word of God, and go out witnessing with the new convert. For a month, it was just the two of them, but soon a small group of Helen's classmates joined their afternoon meetings.

Many were affected. One of Helen's teachers at Holy Cross College was sick with a fever and asked Helen to pray for her. When Helen prayed, the fever left instantly!

I continued to speak at the college amidst the activist atmosphere. The newspapers carried stories of the continuing street fighting in Manila between students with stones and Molotov cocktails and police with tear gas. In class I was asked whether the revolution of Jesus Christ was the militant one they were seeking. I assured them it was not.

One night after a class in which I had spoken, activists on campus challenged Helen about her position. What followed was a lively conversation in the regional dialect of Visayan. Helen held her own as she stood firmly for Christ in a spirited fashion. Listening in the background, Rey Yap observed it all.

Rey continued to visit us and often climbed the stairs to our "apartment" above the church. A keen musician, he was eager to learn our songs and share his own. He listened attentively as Graeme and Margaret sang their harmonized duets. He also began joining our regular Saturday evening beach trips. During these fellowship times, we swam and played games on the sand until we collapsed in laughter or exhaustion. Ever faithful, Mike would roast hot dogs as methodically as he kept our financial records. Graeme would keep us entertained with his humor and songs. After dark we sang by the light of the fire, with Rey occasionally strumming a guitar.

On weekdays, we continued our witnessing, preaching, and praying. I knew this was the kind of work God had given us to do— the good works He had prepared for us. Other doors were open, too, and Mike would often take the bus to the nearby town of Tagum to preach. Mike was not a talker, but he did share with us how well the meetings were going.

"They really seem to enjoy what I have to say," he said quietly. What remarkable development there had been in this shy young man's life during the time he had been serving on a team.

One Sunday morning, a student activist in Davao named Jack questioned me outside the church. He disagreed with the sermon I had just preached. Committed to Marxism, he saw communism as the only answer to the rampant corruption in the Philippines. I tried to reason with him, but I knew I was making contact with neither his mind or his heart. Suddenly a thought occurred to me.

"Suppose we were to take all the wealth of the Philippines and pile it in a heap," I suggested, "and divide it equally among everyone in the country. Would that solve all the woes of this nation caused by corruption?"

Jack looked at me but said nothing. A little later he excused himself and left. After he had gone, I mused on that thought that seemingly had come from nowhere. Was this another answer to our around-the-clock prayers?

A few days later I saw Jack again. His attitude was completely different.

"I went home after our talk the other morning," he told me, "and began searching for a communist answer to your question. I knew that the redistribution of wealth would not stop rampant personal evil in our country. I wrestled all day with that problem until 11 p.m. But I couldn't sleep, I tossed and turned until 2 a.m. Finally, I realized I should yield my life to Christ. Doing that made more sense than giving my life to communism."

And so Jack joined the group of new converts—Helen and Virgie and a young man named Mat. Others joined the growing group one by one. Rey continued to visit us, sing our songs, and accompany us to the beach on Saturday nights. But he still held out against giving his life to Christ. For him the price was too high. We had stressed to him from Proverbs 28:13 that coming to Christ meant more than just *confessing* his sins. God required him to *forsake* them. That meant turning from everything he knew was wrong, but Rey had sins he wasn't ready to give up.

After we'd been in Davao for two months, we were to attend a conference of YWAM leaders in New Zealand. With so much happening at the church, we weren't eager to leave Davao, but we felt we should attend the conference. Kel Steiner, an invaluable member of our team during the previous year in Asia, agreed to come down from Manila to lead the group in my absence. Kel was an outstanding personal worker who would spend hours with anyone interested in the gospel. He often led people to Christ. I so admired this quality in him and told him all about Rey.

While we were in New Zealand, Kel wrote me that just days after Margaret and I had left, he'd spent an afternoon sharing the gospel with Rey. One night after Kel had preached in our storefront church, Rey finally saw himself as God saw him in his sin, and he came weeping to the altar. Amidst tears of repentance he embraced the forgiveness that only Jesus gives!

When Margaret and I returned to Davao, we were thrilled to greet Rey as a brother in Christ and not just as a friend. Rey now faithfully attended services and asked us to continue to place benches on the footpath outside so that passersby could sit and listen to the gospel. On more than one occasion, he pointed to one of our wooden benches and said, "If it weren't for a bench like that, I would never have come to Christ!"

After our three-month commitment to the church was over, Margaret and I decided to stay for a while longer. Kel returned to his work in the north. Some of our team members also stayed in Davao for another five months. By the time Margaret and I went to Europe to undergo further missionary training, we had left a solid core of young people who were the envy of other churches.

Postscript

A few years ago I returned to Davao, twenty-one years after the events just described. Jack was pastoring the very church outside of which we had talked that day in 1972 and was reaching out in a valuable ministry to college students. He told me, "If I hadn't come to Christ then, I'd now be a communist commander in the bush, or dead." Rey told me about his ministry at a Christian school. And Helen and her husband were traveling the Philippines, teaching on intercession, an appropriate ministry for someone who was brought to the Lord as a result of prayer.

Although it was God's will that we worked with that church for those months, we could not have folded our arms, done nothing, and waited for God to show up. James (the brother of Jesus) tells us that "faith by itself, if it is not accompanied by action is dead" (James 2:17). This doesn't mean that we should engage in frenzied activity. Such activity sometimes indicates that we are like trees just sprouting leaves rather than bearing fruit. Some Christians can be very impressed with "leaves" because they give the appearance of achieving something. But the Lord isn't impressed: "By their fruit you will recognize them" (Matt. 7:16).

Our faith should lead to works, but we must make sure they are Spirit-led activities. God obviously had led us to pray "and not give Him any rest." Looking back, I can see that it was our around-the-clock prayer vigil that helped us to give birth to the fruit we saw. But the witnessing and preaching were also works God used.

In some parts of the world, such as the Philippines, it is not hard to draw large numbers to a Christian meeting and then to see many respond to the call to give their lives to Christ. Spiritually aware in the first place, these people quickly respond to such appeals. But lasting conversions are another story. Reflecting on the events in Davao all those years ago, I have learned a valuable lesson about faith: that without works it is dead. In Davao, God had led us to witness and to preach as we prayed around the clock.

Looking back, something else has come into focus. We had stopped the 24-hour prayer vigil after two months, since we needed to take a break at that time. But I wonder what would have happened if we had resumed it. All the notable lasting conversions described in this chapter relate directly to those first two months during which we gave God no rest.

I've heard it said that the world belongs to the disciplined. It's also true that walking in faith requires discipline. When we receive a word from God, it often does not come to pass unless we persevere. Matthew 14:25-31 illustrates this well. Peter received a word from Jesus to walk on the water, but he lost faith after turning his attention away from Jesus and toward the crashing waves and howling winds. How like Peter we all are!

To teach me more about the importance of discipline and perseverance in faith, the Lord arranged just the right set of circumstances. Over the years, He has called me to do some radical things, but few have tested my faith as much as the time He directed me to go to Manado in northern Indonesia.

CHAPTER FOUR

Never Give Up!

Margaret and I had finished six months of missionary training in Europe and were looking forward to returning to the Philippines with our newborn son Mark. While on an overnight visit to Copenhagen, a friend and I started talking about Asia and were soon perusing a map of the region. Suddenly, my friend pointed to a region of Indonesia just south of the Philippines. Circling Manado with his finger he said, "Many Christians live in this area."

I couldn't believe my ears. "But I spent two months traveling and speaking in Indonesia a few years ago," I protested. "I found it to be a very Muslim country!"

"Yes, but in Manado it is very different. There are many Christians there."

The next day as I traveled by road through falling snow, a thought slipped into my mind that was thousands of miles from my icy surroundings. It came with such peace, clarity, and authority that I never doubted it was from God: *When you return to the Philippines you are to take teams to Manado.*

෯ ෯ ෯ ෯

That word from the Lord was uppermost in my mind when I

left Margaret and our son Mark in Baguio (BAH-ghee-oh) and flew into Davao on an early June morning in 1973. In my briefcase were my passport and newly taken photographs I'd need for an Indonesian visa application.

Finding a plane was my first concern. In 1973 there was no scheduled direct airline service between Davao and Manado, even though the Indonesian city was a mere 300 miles away. To get to Manado by airliner you had to fly to Manila and then through Singapore to Jakarta. The next day you would fly through Ujang Pandang and on to Manado. A circuitous, expensive two-day trip!

All concerns about my travel dissipated as I stepped from the plane in Davao to be greeted by the familiar sight of Mt. Apo and smiling friends. The warm welcome I received later from Rey, Helen, Jack, and the others made me wish Margaret and Mark were with me. Margaret and I had come to love these young people so much!

My missionary friends introduced me to the storefront church's new pastor, who invited me to lead a week of special meetings. During that week of preaching, I heard that a Bouraq Indonesian airliner had been chartered for a trip to Manado and was to depart right after my final meeting. Excitedly, I prayed about it and felt I should try to get on board. These rare flights were a new phenomenon that occurred when Filipino loggers were employed in the lush tropical forests of Indonesia.

Even if I were to find a way to get on board, I had no guarantee of a flight to bring me back. This was a big stumbling block for the Indonesian consulate official who wanted to see tickets before granting a visa. Of course, I could supply none. The only flights were these unpredictable chartered ones, sometimes months apart. Besides, I didn't have any money for a round-trip ticket.

Then an idea struck me.

"There's talk of a possible return flight in ten days' time," I told the doubting consulate official. "If I can get a letter from the agents, Air Manila, would that do?

The official agreed that it would. I hurried to see the Air Manila manager, who knew me from my time in the city the previous year. He listened attentively as I described the letter I needed and then reached for his company's stationery.

"Here, use one of these. That flight in ten days' time is not for sure, but you can write what you want and I'll sign it!"

"Really?" I responded, feeling encouraged. "Then I'll take some with me and come back this afternoon!"

Back in my room, I struggled to type the letter, which was tricky to write. How could I say what the consul wanted to hear, word the letter in a way that the Air Manila manager would take responsibility for, and be truthful? I scratched my chin and squinted at what I wrote many times before I finished the assignment to the satisfaction of my conscience.

That afternoon I spoke once more with the consulate official, who looked at my visa application and seemed satisfied with the manager's letter on airline stationery.

"What about your funds?" he asked. "How much are you going to take in?"

My heart sank. This was the question I had been dreading. I couldn't promise to take in a penny. I tried to sound confident.

"How much would you want me to take in?"

"Ten dollars a day," was his reply.

Ten dollars a day was a lot of money to people living in the Philippines in 1973. And to me. I could ride in a bus for five hours for less than a dollar!

"Ten dollars a day," I said thoughtfully as I did some calculating. "That would mean $100 for ten days."

I did not mean to imply that I would be taking in $100. I was merely doing my mathematics aloud. But for some reason, the consul stopped asking me questions and didn't ask to see any traveler's checks. He jotted something down on a piece of paper and told me to return later for the visa.

I was ecstatic. As I rode home on a colorfully decorated "jeepney"—an elongated jeep that provides public transport in the Philippines—I began to face my situation realistically. To have a visa was one thing. To get back from Indonesia when no flights were guaranteed was quite another! I was a father now, with responsibilities to my family and others.

If returning presented a problem, so did leaving. I still needed to get a seat on Monday's flight. For that to happen, I needed permission from whichever logging company was chartering the flight.

The business affairs had been conducted in Indonesia, and because of the lack of telecommunications between Mindanao and Indonesia, the details were unknown to Air Manila.

Still, I had walked this path before. Perseverance, I'd found, was the key once you'd heard from God. The conviction to make this trip had been real for so long.

I awoke at 5:30 a.m. on Monday morning to get to the airport early, as the Air Manila manager had suggested. The airport bustled with more-than-normal activity with the green and white Bouraq Indonesian airliner sitting on the tarmac. I nervously paced, waiting to see whether I could take the flight. Finally, the manager called me over.

"I've talked to the people involved in chartering the airliner, and they are allowing you to fly," he explained kindly.

I paid $45 for the ticket, leaving just $7 in Philippine currency in my thin wallet. Just before 7 a.m., I walked out with the other passengers onto the tarmac bathed in beautiful morning sunshine. I had no return ticket, no guarantee of a flight, and no money to pay for a ticket should there be a plane. But I was off to Manado!

As our Avro propeller-driven plane banked its wings and headed in an unfamiliar southerly direction, the reality of what I was doing sunk in. I knew no one in Manado. And what would I say if the airport officials wanted to see a return ticket or asked me how much money I was carrying?

I was hoping to get to speak publicly on this trip as I investigated further opportunities. But I knew I would receive few, if any, gifts as a result of preaching. Any money coming my way would have to be through the hands of an individual inspired by God or some other miraculous way. Even the $7 in Philippine currency in my wallet could be worthless, as it was often not convertible in other countries. A wave of negative emotions kept assailing me. I felt like an astronaut on a rocket that had no ability to return to earth!

Once the "Fasten Seat Belt" sign had been switched off, I walked down the aisle of the small plane, asking the few people on board whether they knew of any other way back to Davao. Perhaps by boat? But no one could help. I returned to my seat and resigned myself to prayer.

Years earlier on the Indonesian island of Java, someone had given me the name of a Manado church. I pulled out my address book, looked up the church and decided that it was my only possible hope upon arrival. I struck up a conversation with the steward on board the flight, and later showed him the address of the church.

"I know where that is," he volunteered. "You can ride in the airline car with us after we arrive."

That was encouraging.

After about an hour and a half in the air, the pilot announced our descent into Manado, and soon we skimmed over the endless rows of coconut trees. After we'd touched down, I made my way into the arrival area and instantly recognized the clove-scented smoke of Indonesian cigarettes. This familiar aroma brought back a rush of nostalgic memories from our team's visit to Java, a thousand miles away, the year Margaret and I were married.

I handed my passport to the immigration officer on duty, who eyed it carefully.

"What's your occupation?" he asked sternly.

I thought he might be more friendly if I used some Indonesian I'd picked up on that outreach three years earlier.

"*Guru,*" I replied. Teacher.

But my idea was ill-advised. Perhaps inspired by my knowledge of Indonesian, he continued to ask me questions.

"What kind of teacher are you?" he continued coolly.

"*Guru agama*" I said, remembering the correct phrase for a religious teacher.

"Well, you won't teach while you are here!" He then pounded the entry stamp onto my passport with an air of finality.

I walked slowly away from the counter, feeling suddenly sick at heart. *What on earth am I doing in Manado? What am I going to do with myself if I can't preach?*

My only answer to that question was to persevere in the way God had led me. In the military you always obey the last command given. I was learning that in God's army you do the same. I had no option but to continue in faith and believe in the guidance God had given.

The airport was quite a distance from town, so I was grateful for the ride in the Bouraq Airline's crew car. I craned my neck to see the sights. This was Indonesia all right. I could see the distinctive baked orange tiles on the roofs as we passed the houses. Once in the city, those ever-present tiles stood out even more. At the church, the driver pulled into a big parking lot, and the steward jumped out to unload my bag. As the car eased its way out of the lot and onto the street, I turned to look at the church building. What I'd heard in Europe really was true! There must be many Christians in this area. Slowly I approached an open door.

Inside the vestibule, several young people met me. Forced to use my broken Indonesian, I explained who I was and why I was in Manado. I was told to take a seat and wait.

Before long, I was taken to another church of the same denomination several blocks away. It, too, was a sizable building. After a few minutes, I faced a young Australian missionary about my age.

"Ross Tooley," he repeated slowly. "I've heard of you."

Me? How could anyone have heard of me in this middle-of-nowhere-place! But he interrupted my thoughts.

"Could you preach tonight?"

"But..." I stammered, "but...they told me at the airport I couldn't!"

"Give me your passport. We have church members in the immigration office who will validate everything."

My heart leaped. This was getting better. Perseverance was paying off. I was soon introduced to Pastor Han and his wife, a delightful Chinese-Indonesian couple in their sixties. They immediately made me feel at home, and Pastor Han confirmed the invitation to speak at his church that evening. Mrs. Han made a bed for me in a spare room in their house, which was part of the church building. The room with its cement floor contained little more than a steel bed, a wooden chair, and a dresser, but it was like heaven to me. After lunch I gratefully napped. I preached that night and felt completely at home with the church members who had come to eat with us at the manse after the service. What an incredible week it had been.

The next evening Pastor Han took me to yet another church, where I was to speak for two evenings. At the first meeting, I spoke on the cross of Christ and why His cruel death was necessary for the forgiveness of our many sins. Halfway through the sermon, the interpreter began to cry, and I noticed other people in the congregation weeping. God was really moving!

During our spicy meal of fish, rice, and vegetables after the service, Pastor Han spoke through an interpreter so that I could fully understand his words.

"Next time you come to Manado," he said, looking very serious, "bring your wife. I'll pay her airfare!"

What irony! I had no money to get home from even this trip. But I said nothing. I was convinced I didn't need to mention my financial needs. In the past seven years as a missionary, I had drawn no salary. Margaret and I had our financial ups and downs to be sure, but God was providing. We'd been married four years and had traveled extensively. We were a little family now, and when Mark was born, the Swiss hospital bill had been enormous. But soon after Mark's birth, God supplied the funds needed through a totally surprising channel. I just knew God would provide for me even in this developing country without my saying anything.

I was encouraged by what had happened in just two days. People were clearly responding to the preaching. I learned that the area around Manado had many born-again Christians. The area had been a stronghold of the Dutch in colonial days, and because of the Dutch influence, most of the population was at least nominally Christian.

This was a rare phenomenon in Muslim Indonesia and contrasted sharply with Java, where Margaret and I and the team of thirty-five young people had ministered in 1969-70. If I could just motivate Christians in Manado, I reasoned, the gospel would impact other areas. Manado church leaders were telling me that no one had ever come to teach them on personal evangelism!

I was also heartened on a another score. In Manado I noticed a practice I'd not seen elsewhere in Indonesia. At every meeting, a second offering was taken for the guest speaker. That offering (sometimes wrapped in newspaper) often consisted of the equivalent of dimes, nickels, and pennies, but it added up. After three services, I had about $15 in local currency toward my return airfare. But there still weren't any flights!

On the fourth day of my stay in Manado, with no meetings scheduled, I contacted the Bouraq office. They had no word about a plane to Davao. I tried the shipping companies. The only sea vessel anyone had heard of sailing to Davao was a barge carrying cement. But even that had been discontinued. My ten-day visa was fast running out, and I still had no way to return to Davao.

The Lord was the only one I could look to. The telecommunications systems at that time made it difficult to think of calling Margaret, and she wouldn't have had any spare money to send anyway. I had no credit card to buy a ticket via the expensive route back through Singapore even if I wanted to return that way.

On my fifth day I was taken to the port settlement of Bitung to preach at a five-day series of meetings. Halfway through the meetings, a report reached me that a Bouraq flight was going to Davao on Thursday, the last day of my visa. If this were true, I had to get on board! I bumped along the road on the first available minibus into Manado to find out. To my surprise, the steward I had befriended was working in the airline office when I arrived. He confirmed the report and said that I could take the flight!

All I needed was the $45 for the fare! I had no idea how the offerings were going in my present series of meetings. Bitung was only a country town. In any event, God was not limited to providing in that way. On the final evening, my new friends in Manado, including Pastor Han, came to take me back for the next day's flight. As I was saying goodbye, someone gave me a package wrapped in newspaper. I knew it would be the offerings, and I gratefully stuffed the package into my pants pocket.

As I climbed into the front seat of the car with Pastor Han, weariness suddenly overcame me. It was past midnight before we made it back to home, and by then I was too exhausted to even put up the mosquito net. I collapsed on the bed fully clothed and instantly fell asleep.

It was already light when I awoke to the sound of diesel jeeps chugging away on the road outside the Hans' house. Groggily, I arose and was suddenly aware that this was the day I was supposed to return to the Philippines. I thrust my hand into my pocket and pulled out the package I had slept on all night. Slowly I counted all the small denominations of money over and over, but each time I still came up $5 short.

Then I remembered the $7 in Philippine currency in my wallet. Would the banks convert Philippine money in a place like this? Suddenly I remembered hearing Pastor Han talk one day about visiting Davao. I decided to ask him if he could change the money into Indonesian currency. He readily agreed, and I dashed off to buy my ticket.

At Manado airport, I gratefully pumped the hands of many friends who had come to see me off. As I said goodbye, I didn't know I would be landing at this airport another five times over the next six years.

That eventful trip had one more surprise left. As I climbed aboard the YS-11 sixty-seat propeller plane bound for Davao, on my way back to Baguio and my family, I realized something quite strange. I was the only passenger!

Postscript

Later that afternoon, the plane touched down in Davao. I disembarked immensely thankful to God for the ministry of the past ten days and for the fulfillment of what He had told me to do.

Once back in Baguio, I described my trip to Graeme Jones and Kel Steiner. Within months they were preaching in services set up by Pastor Han, ministering not only in Manado but also in the mountain area nearby.

Eventually, a small team from the Philippines taught, preached, and sang nightly in many meetings. Then in 1977, I had a remarkable time of ministry in and around Manado when a large denomination was experiencing a crisis. Over a twenty-one-day period, I was called upon to speak each night in church buildings so packed that people sometimes stood outside the windows to listen. My schedule included a week of meetings in the church building where the Bouraq Airline car had first taken me when I arrived in 1973. A thousand people attended those meetings every night.

While I have had further outstanding times of ministry in other places, that 1977 trip remains the best three weeks of preaching I've ever had! During my many trips to Manado, I have preached in towns throughout the hill country area as far as Amurung in one direction and to the islands of Sanghir in the other.

Perseverance

Although my last trip to Indonesia was fourteen years ago, I look fondly back on that trip in 1973 when perseverance paid handsome dividends for the kingdom of God. A key element in performing exploits in faith is perseverance. It took many years of perseverance for Joseph to see the dream he had at age 17 fulfilled by becoming prime minister of Egypt. Steadfastness kept him going when he was cruelly sold into slavery and when he was imprisoned unjustly for righteously standing against the lustful advances of Potiphar's wife (Gen. 39:10-13).

Perseverance propelled Moses from the burning bush to the doors of the promised land. It took him through the difficulties of dealing with a stubborn Pharaoh and the unbelievable faithlessness of the Israelites as they traveled the barren desert.

Persistence took Elijah from the time he heard God to watching the defeat of the prophets of Baal.

All three men of God had their moments of testing and weakness, and even of failure. But that is what makes them champions. They were mortal. They became discouraged, and they despaired of life. But they kept going. The book of Proverbs says, "Though a righteous man falls seven times, he rises again" (Prov. 24:16). God looks for that kind of determination in us. Continuance in the face of adversity distinguishes effective Christians from ordinary ones. Many of us, I fear, give up just a stone's throw from victory.

When we have a word from the Lord, as discussed in the introduction to this book, we can completely trust God. Just as Peter had the assurance to step out onto the deep (Matt. 14:28-29), we, too, can launch into the unknown with a word from Christ. My ability to persevere with the trip to Manado lay only in my conviction that God had spoken.

Having a word from the Lord is not enough, however. We must not abandon that word. How prone we are, all of us, to do so when the going gets tough. How easy it was for Peter to submit to the howling wind and choppy Sea of Galilee and desert Jesus' word. We also will sink if we take our eyes off the Lord.

In the end, Peter became an outstanding example for us to follow. History tells us that he served God faithfully to his final day, choosing the agony of crucifixion over denying the faith. That is certainly a challenge for us all.

What is the goal God has put into your heart? You will reach it if you persist. For Joseph, it was to be the leader God intended him to be. For Moses, it was to safely transport people to the promised land. For Elijah, it was the exaltation of the true God and the destruction of the prophets of Baal. Once you have your goal in sight, then stick to it. Persevere! (1 Cor. 15:58).

Although Moses had a word from God to take the children of Israel out of Egypt, he still encountered setbacks along the way. As I read about his many confrontations with the Pharaoh, I am struck by this thought: At every barrier he continued in obedience to God, resulting in a greater victory at a later date.

If we are faithful in following God's directions, we can trust Him with the results. I wish I had understood this principle of faith before I experienced the following episode.

CHAPTER FIVE

Obey God and Leave the Results to Him

Shortly after my return to Davao from Indonesia, the Lord directed Margaret and me to shift our ministry focus to the northern Philippine city of Baguio. Most missionaries would jump at such an assignment. Situated high in the mountains of northern Luzon, the city's cool temperature and pine-scented forests contrast sharply with the tropical humidity and rice paddies of the lowlands. But because of our friendships in Davao, I wasn't eager to relocate. My heart belonged down south. And so it was only slowly that I began to warm to the idea of permanently settling in Baguio.

Our bus to Baguio zigged and zagged up the narrow mountain road, perilously close to the sheer cliffs. But at the end of the trip we were generously rewarded with the sight of a sweeping panorama of pine trees. At the elevation of 5,000 feet, Margaret and I and our son Mark were immediately invigorated by the cooler climate. It was as though we'd arrived in a different country.

We were greeted by our friend Kel, who had spearheaded the beginning of the YWAM Baguio center but who was now wanting to return to New Zealand. It was our privilege to carry on the work of this ministry and seek God for further direction. We were a company of twenty YWAM staff that included our good friends Mike Shelling and Graeme Jones. Mike was as conscientious as ever, keeping the accounts and ministering faithfully one on one to a steady stream of Filipinos. Graeme, now sporting a red beard, kept us laughing at his jokes and singing his songs.

With a 1973 population of only 125,000, Baguio boasted four universities and one college. It wasn't long before God gave Margaret and me a ministry among the students. I was thoroughly enjoying the opportunities to reach out to the thousands of youths drawn from Baguio and the surrounding provinces. Before long we started regular gatherings in our house that attracted up to ninety students at a time. Graeme and Margaret teamed up again musically, and many of us took turns to preach. Graeme and Mike had developed into effective preachers, as had Sammy Tenizo and Paul Filler, two young Filipinos on our staff. The students loved these meetings in the YWAM house, which, because of its color, they affectionately called the "Pink House." To meet the spiritual hunger of the students, Margaret and other team members started discipleship classes that met regularly during the week.

From our large three-storied house, we sent out evangelistic teams to both lowland and highland peoples. It was among the highlanders living higher up on the picturesque terraced mountainsides that Mike really felt at home. He began to dream of settling up there permanently.

We all engaged in the ministry of intercession for both local and international problems. One day in 1974 we received an urgent request from a missionary group in Manila asking us to join them in a prayer and letter-writing campaign against *The Exorcist*, a movie that openly glorified terrifying demon power.

Our staff immediately started praying that the film would be banned from the Philippines, and we fired off telegrams to both the board of censors and President Ferdinand Marcos. We hadn't received any "writing in the sky" orders to do this. It was just that after praying I was at peace about our actions. Based on my understanding of God's character, I felt it was right to oppose such spiritual evil.

Despite our stance and the fact that the Philippines is a predominantly Roman Catholic nation, the national board passed the movie. In contrast, the board of censors of neighboring Muslim Indonesia did the exact opposite and banned it. Ironically, it couldn't agree with the devil prevailing against the cross!

When we heard that the film would soon be opening in Baguio, we asked Mayor Luis Lardizarbal to take a stand against it. In an unusual turn of events, Merry Towle (a staff member from Minneapolis) and Mike Shelling were invited to a special preview of *The Exorcist* with the local board of censors. Our YWAMers were horrified by its blatant anti-Christian content.

The local censors saw things differently, however. Mayor Lardizarbal countered by ruling that entrance was to be limited to those 21 and over. Some members of the board insisted that the age of admission be 18. The mayor, who was endowed with a dogmatism uncommon in the Philippines, was just as adamant to keep it at 21. It was a small victory. Or so we thought.

Despite the mayor's ruling, our student friends reported that many under 21 were pouring into the theater. I spoke with the mayor, who ruled that if we wished, we could check people's ages as they entered the theater. Did we really want to go to this much trouble? I didn't think so. But to my surprise, when I took it up with the team at the next prayer time, they felt we should!

Crowds of young people continued to turn up to see the film. But they were greeted by age restriction signs and our staff checking IDs. Only a trickle were now permitted to enter the cinema.

One morning, Fred Sanchez, a Filipino staff member, called from the theater, his voice strained and anxious.

"There's a riot here," he said. "You'd better come right away!"

I could hear the noise of the crowd in the background, and I groaned silently.

"Okay, I'll come," I said reluctantly, slowly replacing the receiver. For a moment I stared vacantly at the black, well-worn telephone. What was I getting myself into! Not sure what to expect, I walked the few blocks to the theater, skirting Baguio's Burnham Park with its man-made lake and surrounding green lawns.

The crowds had scattered when I arrived, but I took in a smoldering silence. The theater manager threw me especially dark looks. We were turning away 90 percent of the potential moviegoers. This was more than the theater people could take, and several days later they tore down the signs and drove our workers away. As far as the management was concerned, it was business as usual.

Back at the Pink House the team prayed about our next move. Should we drop our protest or continue to challenge the theater owner? I felt I should at least bring the mayor up to date. After hearing my report, he arranged a time for me to meet with him and the theater owner. At one point in the meeting, the owner fixed his cold eye on me and said: "If you press this and we continue to lose patronage, I'll sue you and your group."

Legally he had a good case. Since the film had passed both the national and the local boards of censors, he had every right to show it. The mayor's age ruling was legally just a recommendation. But we are living under martial law, and a Marcos-backed mayor wielded a lot of power. I didn't know the theater had legal cause. I just knew by the hostile tone of the owner's voice that I didn't want to tangle with him.

After the owner had left, the mayor asked me what our next step would be. I told him I thought we had gone far enough, thanked him for his help, and left. Although it was only a short walking distance to the Pink House, it was a long, painful journey. What would I tell the team? Some of them would be very disappointed. But, ever an optimist, I tried thinking of all the good that had been accomplished. Yet deep down I wondered whether it had been worth all the time and effort expended. I put on a brave face as I shared the news with the team. But all the while I was thinking, *We sure wouldn't want to do this again!*

ⅆ ⅆ ⅆ ⅆ

That chapter of our lives seemed mostly forgotten in the busy activity of the next two years. We continued to work with the university students, sharing the gospel with them in Burnham Park, their dorms, and even classrooms. We were delighted as many came to the Lord. Student meetings that we held each Friday and Sunday were also well attended.

Because few YWAM centers dotted the Asian landscape in those days, the visit from an international YWAM leader in an isolated outpost like ours was a major event. When Lynn Green, then director of YWAM England, visited the Philippines, it was a joy to hear him speak at our student meeting.

Lynn is a keen sportsman, and wanting to make him as welcome as possible, I invited him to try his hand at *pelota*, a popular local game similar to racquetball. As our faithful jeep bumped along the rutted road to the courts, Lynn chatted about his time in Auckland, New Zealand, just before coming to see us.

"I had a couple of hours to spare one day," he said, "and I felt prompted to see *The Omen*."

"Oh!" I replied with some surprise. I had heard of the film, which was said to be very similar to *The Exorcist*.

"It's a terrible film," he continued. "It teaches evil is supreme and cannot be stopped. It also focuses unnecessarily on horrific injuries."

My heart sank. This movie was due to be shown soon throughout the Philippines. I recalled our losing battle with *The Exorcist*, and I groaned inwardly at the thought of facing another bad influence.

At the pelota courts, Lynn and I were soon engaged in a hard game. As I chased Lynn's shots, my mind returned to our conversation in the jeep. In contesting the showings of *The Exorcist*, I was at a constant disadvantage with the critics who challenged me, since one of my handicaps was that I had never seen the film.

"How do you know this movie is evil if you haven't even seen it?" people would ask.

The tone of their voice declared how illogical they thought I was. I saw their point. But Lynn had seen *The Omen*. What if he were to talk to the mayor about it...

Well, it couldn't happen, I tried to tell myself. I really didn't want to get involved again. Besides, it was late Friday afternoon, and by the time we'd have finished the game and gone home to shower, it would be too late. The mayor would not be in his office, and Lynn would be safely on his way to England before Monday.

We continued to slam and dive for the ball. I was impressed by Lynn's agility, but I was more bothered by an inner voice that spoke as we played.

Take Lynn to the mayor's office right now.

I wrestled with the thought. Surely God wouldn't want us to visit the mayor dressed in our tennis whites and gym shoes! And since I didn't want a repeat of *The Exorcist* debacle, I tried to shake off the impression and continued playing. But that voice wouldn't leave.

When the game ended, I slowly walked to the side of the court, stopped and prayed intensely under my breath for a moment. Nothing would budge that thought! *Well, I'll see what Lynn thinks about it.*

He didn't bat an eye.

"Sure, I'll go with you!"

We piled into the open jeep, and I drove to City Hall. Because we could not lock the jeep, we appeared before Mayor Lardizarbal not only wearing our sweat-soaked playing regalia but also carrying our pelota rackets.

Despite our odd apparel, the mayor listened intently as Lynn described the movie. When Lynn had finished, the mayor promised he would recommend that it not screen in Baguio. We left, grateful to God for His leading. There had hardly been a battle. Perhaps we were being rewarded for all the hassles we'd endured opposing *The Exorcist.*

As I walked down the steps of City Hall, my spirit soared. I was confident the film would not show. Whew, that had been easy!

Several weeks passed before I learned how naive I was. Scanning the Sunday paper one day, I noticed an announcement about a sneak preview of *The Omen*—scheduled that week at the Pines Theater. My mouth went dry. Oh, no, here we go again!

Because of the mayor's negative recommendation, the local board of censors needed to view the movie. I asked the mayor for permission to accompany them, and I asked our ministry team to cover me in prayer as I subjected myself to the ordeal.

It felt strange taking a seat in a large theater with so few others. The sparsity of the audience seemed to draw attention to the gravity of the job at hand. During the first hour of the movie I felt embarrassed. What was there to protest? I quickly changed my mind as I watched demon powers release the emergency brake of a truck carrying glass. The resulting decapitation scene was grue-some. The movie's hideous message became clearer as the film pro-gressed. Lynn was right. It left viewers feeling that evil was supreme.

Although it was evident to me that *The Omen* was harmful, members of the censors' board disagreed. Despite my protests, they passed the film. I did, however, get the promise of one letter from a board member who preferred that the film not be shown.

I began to secure other letters of opposition. One was from the Roman Catholic bishop of Baguio who readily backed my position. The film was already showing in Manila and other cities where it was attracting unhealthy attention.

The editor of one of Baguio's newspapers had attended the pre-view and wrote a review, commenting on our protest. I requested equal space to reply. Graciously, the paper published my review in which I explained why it was important for Christians to oppose the film's destructive message.

Finally, as a result of many letters of protest, the management of the Pines Theater decided not to screen the film. We were delighted! Our joy turned to dismay several weeks later, however, when a theater on a side street in Baguio began advertising it. Despite our appeals to the theater, the film still showed.

Once again, I began to question the value of the countless hours I had spent opposing these evil movies. All that effort. All that prayer. All those letters gathered. All the running around. All that time with the mayor.

Were there any lasting results? It was true that fewer people saw *The Omen* in that side street movie house than might have other-wise seen it. And as a result of our protests to the second theater, the manager did concede one point. He could understand our opposi-tion to a coming attraction showing a demented priest about to strangle a girl with a rosary. When I took that subject up with the mayor, he barked out the order for an aide to get the manager on the phone. As I listened to his every word, the mayor told the man-ager he'd padlock the premises if he dared screen the movie. Fortunately, the film did not show during all my years in Baguio. That, at least, was one little victory.

Leave the Consequences to God

An early lesson we learn about faith is that our job is to love and obey God. We are not responsible for the outcome of our obedience if we but do His will with the right attitude. We must leave the consequences with Him.

It's true that at times we have little or even nothing to show for our obedience. Whenever this happens, it gives God a wonderful opportunity to teach us meekness.

So important to our faith is humility that Jesus charged the Pharisees with unbelief because they lacked this virtue. "How can you believe," He asked them one day, "if you accept praise from one another, yet make no effort to obtain the praise that comes from...God?" (John 5:44).

The Lord in His wisdom knows the failing of the human heart when it comes to pride. He works on this wretched aspect of our fallen nature throughout our entire lives. And so we learn the value of the saying, "Nothing succeeds like failure." At times, to purify our hearts, God deliberately lets us see nothing for our efforts. He wants us to continue in faith for His glory, not for the thrill of the results to make us look good in the eyes of others.

When we know we have received a word from God, we are simply to obey. Whether things go well or not is not our primary concern. If things don't go well, God uses the circumstance to help sanctify us.

The eleventh chapter of Hebrews boasts examples of spiritual giants accomplishing their goals, but it also points to another group of faith heroes: those who obeyed God but didn't achieve what they aimed for. The writer concluded: "These were all commended for their faith, yet none of them received what had been promised" (Heb. 11:39).

Sometimes it is a matter of timing. There is a schedule for the results to manifest themselves. God controls that schedule. In Baguio we didn't see what we expected or wanted. Yet in the spiritual realm, I believe that through obedience, prayer, and faith, victories took place that we didn't see immediately.

We were soon to learn what these victories were.

Motivated by love, men and women work harder than they ever would for money. In the spiritual realm, God has always intended that all our actions be motivated by His love, including our exploits in faith. That's why the Bible explains that faith works by love (Gal. 5:6).

Love energizes our faith. When we love God and trust in His unchanging character, we gain courage to step out in obedience. Love is especially critical in our ministry to individuals and nations. When we receive a true revelation of God's love, we want to tell others about Him. As I came to really care for the Filipino people, God opened new ways for me to communicate to them—and to reach more people than ever before. Faith made this possible, but love stirred me to action.

Chapter Six

Faith Works by Love

About seventy students crammed into the Pink House in Baguio for the big event. Those who couldn't get a seat, sat on the stairs or stood near the walls. I could sense the expectancy of these college students as they waited to see the movie, or *sine* (pronunced seeneh and short for cinema).

It was almost Christmas in 1974. We had promised we'd show a *sine* called *The Revolution of Love*, the story of 1,000 YWAMers (including Graeme and me) who marched, sang, and witnessed on the streets of Munich during the 1972 Olympic Games. We borrowed an old 16mm projector and hung a sheet on the wall for a screen. Even when the projector caught fire during the screening, the youths weren't dismayed. They eagerly waited for Graeme and his handyman skills to get it operating again.

As we screened the film around the city, I continued to shake my head in wonder about the Filipino's love for movies. In schools and churches, or even in the street, the results were the same: crowds of people with great willingness to stand and watch. They showed patient interest in our message whenever we spoke publicly after a showing. I felt a little ashamed that I'd already been three years in the country and hadn't recognized the immense pulling power a movie had in the Philippines. God clearly was giving us this tool to communicate His love and truth, and I realized I needed to use it.

A year later we gratefully received a film produced by Shira Lindsay called *My Witnesses*. Though it was on the same subject—our involvement at the Munich Olympics—the big difference was its nonreligious scenes, which included clips from the athletic events and amusements outside the Olympic stadium. The film even showed the bombed-out helicopter in which Israeli athletes had been killed by Arab terrorists.

We saw this *sine* as a golden opportunity to reach more Filipinos for Christ. Our little "Youth With A Movie" team made the rounds once more, using a single film and a borrowed projector. Each screening, which further confirmed to us that movies drew Filipinos like a magnet, gave us wonderful opportunities to share the love of God.

When we got our own projector in April 1976, we again began to show *My Witnesses* around the city. To our amazement, the same interest prevailed. After each showing, we joyfully preached, sang, performed dramas, and sold books to the crowds that always appeared—seemingly from nowhere!

Despite these successes, I hadn't fully grasped the potential of our film ministry until we received a letter from Loren Cunningham, YWAM's international president. The letter to all base directors said in part: "If you have a movie, you can offer it to a TV station to broadcast. They will sometimes even pay you for showing it."

I wasn't interested in the money, but my heart leaped at the concept of showing *My Witnesses* over TV. Hundreds had seen our screenings in Baguio, but multiplied *thousands* could see it if it hit the airwaves. The very thought of it set my heart on fire.

Margaret and I had come to deeply love the nation. We wanted more than anything for the people of our adopted homeland to know the Lord, and this would be a great way to reach them.

Regrettably, we were woefully ignorant of the Philippine TV scene. By now we had vacated the Pink House near City Hall and had moved into several smaller dwellings closer to the heart of town. None of our YWAM houses had a TV set, and we didn't know what kind of programs were received in our area. Since there were no stations in Baguio itself, any approach to television would have to be made in Manila, 160 miles away.

A few weeks later I was in my office preparing for just such a trip. Since receiving the letter, a settled persuasion had gripped my heart that God wanted me to offer our film to a TV station. The Montreal Olympic games were just two months away, and a film like ours would be topical.

But which Manila station should we offer it to? Feeling the importance of this decision, I dropped to my knees on the smooth cement office floor. As I sought the Lord for direction, I thought, *Well, I certainly won't be prejudice for or against any station. I didn't know anything!* I had recognized long ago that an essential ingredient in divine guidance was being neutral to what you wanted or thought, and God had made it easy for me this time. Kneeling on my office floor I began to pray:

"Lord, I am trusting you to guide me. Is there anything you want to tell me about which TV station I should approach?"

As I lingered with my eyes closed, a huge letter "K" appeared before my mind's eye. It meant nothing to me, but I hoped it would later.

The next morning I boarded the bus for the five-and-a-half-hour ride. Within minutes of arriving in Manila, I was "walking" with my fingers through the Yellow Pages of the telephone directory. I soon identified five TV stations and to my delight found that only Channel 9 contained a "K" in its call letters. My heart did a little skip when I found out it was Manila's largest TV station.

What time should I approach them, Lord? I had learned that asking God about timing was a wise thing to do. In the Philippines, officials can keep extraordinary hours. Into my head came the thought: *Eleven o'clock tomorrow morning.*

The timing was perfect, and after viewing the film, the station manager agreed to show it one Saturday morning. Although we'd seen the film dozens of times, knew its songs, and could anticipate the next scene, that didn't stop some of us from huddling in front of a TV at a friend's house across town to watch it once more! I had not asked for payment, but I did ask Channel 9 to show our address at the conclusion of the movie so that those interested in its spiritual content could contact us.

When a missionary in charge of a Manila library of sixty Christian films heard what we'd done, he told me, "Ross, if you have an "in" with television, we'll waive the rental fee so you can show any of our films over the air." I was ecstatic!

After that, every time I went to Manila I would swing by the headquarters of Christ for Greater Manila (CGM). Very kindly, they would darken an air-conditioned office, make coffee, and leave me at the controls of a 16mm projector. I was looking for movies that would speak to secular audiences. Two months later, I decided to submit the Billy Graham film *His Land*, starring pop singer Cliff Richard, and Channel 9 agreed to show it.

By this time, Graeme had married Mary Smart in New Zealand, and they had returned to set up their own apartment near us. Above them was an apartment where I could watch the film over TV without having to travel across town. As the movie screened, I distinctly felt God say I should now offer it to Channel 7.

That guidance paid off. Although they didn't show that particular movie, they contacted us a couple of months later saying they needed films to show over the coming Easter week. When asked what other movies we had, I suggested a couple, including the David Wilkerson production, *The Rapture*. Set in the format of a newscast, the film depicts one interpretation of what might be seen over the evening news in the United States just after Christ's return. Channel 7 so loved *The Rapture* that they advertised it all week before showing it during prime time the night before Easter Sunday, 1977.

Once again, the timing was perfect. Many Philippine movie houses were closed for Holy Week, and three of the five TV stations then in existence had closed down, too. We knew we'd have a good audience, but neither Channel 7 nor I was prepared for what happened when the film screened.

Literally millions of Filipinos tuned in to see *The Rapture*. Many thought they were seeing a live satellite broadcast from Washington and that vehicles and aircraft had crashed because drivers and pilots had mysteriously disappeared. Some viewers thought that U.S. President Jimmy Carter and half his cabinet had also vanished! Their alarm could only be heightened by the blank screens on the other channels. The frenzy that night was reminiscent of the famous 1938 radio broadcast, "War of the Worlds," the science fiction program about a Martian landing!

Worried callers jammed the switchboards at Channel 7. Calls flooded the office of the Minister of Information and even the U.S. embassy. Channel 7 scrambled to counteract the hysteria, announcing a disclaimer every fifteen minutes for the next two hours: "The movie you have just seen is only a movie. You have nothing to fear." The station even called in the Minister of Information to broadcast a message to calm the people.

I had no desire to be a fearmonger, but if ever I doubted the power of a movie in the Philippines, it was dispelled that night! Channel 7's staff told us that the audience response to the movie was the biggest the station had ever had. Jarring as it was, the film challenged millions to consider their eternal destiny.

We believe that *The Rapture* set the stage for another major movie thrust. Later in the year, I was once again seated in a darkened office at the CGM library with a movie projector whirring at my elbow. On the screen flashed another Billy Graham movie starring Cliff Richard. *Two a Penny* is the story of a young couple in love at the time of a London Billy Graham crusade. The movie concludes with Dr. Graham preaching for a full five minutes to a packed-out audience and many people coming forward to give their lives to Christ in response to the salvation message.

I was impressed by *Two a Penny*'s message of sexual purity. It grieved me deeply that promiscuity was raging in our university city. In the movie, a young woman named Carol resists the sexual advances of her boyfriend. I knew that this theme was most applicable for Filipino couples in their dating years, and that this film could help address this issue publicly.

As I sat with excitement about presenting the film to a television station, I heard an unmistakable inner voice. This gentle but authoritative voice said, *This movie should be shown in theaters throughout the Philippines.*

The idea took me totally by surprise. I was so focused on television that I never considered theater audiences. But I had to agree. Filipino students were in desperate need of moral guidance, and the movies they flocked to depicted the worst kind of moral values. I was aghast when I heard that the average student went to such movies twice a week. My fear was that these young people would develop a Hollywood morality.

I suddenly felt an inner conviction that the film playing in front of me could help to counteract that. That scene of the young woman slapping the face of her lustful boyfriend needed to hit the big screen! The problem was that in 1977, our 16mm film was too small for big-screen theaters. I pressed Tom, the leader of the film library for a possible solution.

"Tom, that film needs a wider audience. It needs to be shown in every theater in the country!"

"We tried to get several distributors to import 35mm prints for the theater showings," he said. "We even had one distributor agree, but he would never sign the contract."

Tom stopped to ponder the situation for a moment before mentioning something that would alter our entire ministry for the next two years.

"You know, you could show this movie with a 16mm version…," he began

"You mean set a 16mm projector halfway up the aisle of a theater for a public showing?" I interrupted.

I made no attempt to betray my horror at the thought. A friend had tried that during my Bible school days in New Zealand. We had set up a 16mm projector in the aisle, but it produced a pitifully small image on the large theater screen. Tom explained that a special lens could cast an acceptable image on a theater screen—as long as the theater itself was not huge.

I soon learned that I could buy such a lens in Japan. I was planning to go there in a few weeks. When I arrived at the warehouse, however, I was faced with a new dilemma. The lens came in two sizes—and I had no idea which to buy. I had $100 to purchase the lens with in my pocket, but what if I bought the wrong one? A hundred dollars at that time would feed our whole family for over a month. I couldn't bear the thought of wasting that much on a wrong choice, so I left the warehouse.

Once outside, it suddenly occurred to me that God could show me which lens to choose. I bowed my head right there on the street and prayed. Into my head came the impression to buy the smaller of the two sizes offered. I quickly retraced my steps and bought the lens.

Back in Baguio, I couldn't wait to show Graeme the treasured lens. Graeme had once been an auto electrician and was gifted with technical skills that eluded me. I just couldn't imagine launching into any complicated theater showings like this without him. We arranged to try out our prized lens at the Luna Theater late one night.

The question uppermost in my mind as Graeme, Mike, and I climbed the red-carpeted stairs to the projection room was, *Did I get the right size lens?* The three of us worked quickly, as the country was still under martial law and the midnight curfew hour was fast approaching. Once we had everything in place, we let the film roll. An acceptable image flashed before us, and by drawing the curtains a little, it fit nicely on the screen of this smaller-than-usual theater. God had come through again! Rejoicing and relieved, I quickly helped the others pack up. Then with Mike at the wheel, we raced our old Ford back towards the YWAM base.

We were still half a mile away when the curfew siren started wailing. Mike suddenly veered the Ford up a vacant one-way stree—going the wrong way. Graeme threw me a look and then burst into spontaneous laughter. This was so unlike Mike, a model of methodical order. We were going to miss this dear brother. He would be leaving soon for Minnesota to marry another team member, Janice Synstilien. I took a fatherly delight in this turn of events as Margaret and I had encouraged their relationship. We'd miss their help with the movie project, but we were thrilled for them and their future together.

In the days that followed, I mused over the two big problems we faced in our venture. One was simply the question of enough people showing up to see the movie. The other was a technical one. We now had two 16mm projectors, but they were simple ones like those used at social gatherings. With only one special lens, I wondered how we were going to move the lens from one projector to the other without having a blank screen for a time. Philippine theaters often seem to have unruly patrons who rip up the seats if the show is interrupted. What would happen if we couldn't get the lens switched in time?

When I learned that we could rent the Luna Theater for four days, I began to lie awake at night worrying about the possibility of one of our projectors breaking down beyond repair. It would be impossible to operate with just one projector. I called Graeme and Mike and the other leaders together, and we went to prayer asking the Lord whether this was the right film to show in the Luna Theater at this time. Once I knew others felt it was God's will, I stopped worrying.

To get the word out about the film, we approached the director of a local Catholic university. We asked to test the acceptability of the *sine* by showing it to their students and passing out a questionnaire. Sifting through the responses of those young people, I was convinced we should go ahead, but I still questioned whether enough people would see the film. We discussed running showings as a fund-raiser so that all profits above expenses would go to charity. By doing that, we would get a lot of free publicity from the newspapers and radio stations.

Across the street from our girls' house was a home for the blind. The home's leaders were thrilled at our offer to give the proceeds from our *Two a Penny* showings to the home. Margaret's contact with a prominent women's club led the club to throw its support behind the fundraiser. The members sold advance tickets to their friends while we began contacting schools asking teachers to encourage their students to view the movie.

Things had started rolling. Then another way to promote the showings popped into my mind. An honorary board member for the blind home was the Roman Catholic bishop of Baguio whom I'd met while opposing *The Omen* and who had remained a friendly acquaintance. If we were to show him *Two A Penny*, would he endorse it? It was worth a try.

Graeme and I were invited to show the film at the bishop's

palace one night. The audience mainly consisted of nuns in their white habits who quietly watched the movie. When I asked the bishop whether he would endorse the *sine*, he was noncommittal until the nuns started chiming in with their support. As a result, the film showings were announced at every mass for two weeks before the screenings.

I filled Mayor Lardizarbal in on what we were doing. The two newspapers in the city began advertising the showings free of charge. I was already writing a weekly column for one paper, whose editor, a man about my age was particularly helpful. This man published a review of the film I'd written along with one of the still shots from the movie. One day as we sat in a little area that served as the main office of the newspaper company, he leaned back in his wooden chair and made a suggestion.

"Ross, when you show this film of yours for the blind, why don't you suddenly plunge the theater into pitch darkness so that the moviegoers will identify with their plight?"

Knowing that a blank screen might prompt the audience to start ripping at the seats, he suggested we show a slide first that would warn everyone. Although a bit dubious about the idea, I nevertheless ordered the slide.

Five Baguio radio stations gave us free coverage. In the lobby of the Luna Theater under the "Next Attraction" sign hung two beautiful posters the Billy Graham organization had sent us. Our secretaries typed up a letter requesting prayer from most of the fifty YWAM bases then in existence around the world. We were all ready to go.

Or were we? I still worried about the changeover from one reel to the other and the resulting blank screen for a whole minute or two. Any ripped-up seats would be our responsibility. Since we were doing this in the will of God, I said to myself finally, *we'll just have to live with the consequences.*

The first day for the showings arrived. A good contingent from our base was on hand ready to help. We gave Filipino staff members more visible roles, such as selling and collecting tickets, ushering, and passing out the specially prepared brochures that solicited a mail response for those who wanted to know more about the gospel. Rey Yap from Davao was now on our staff, and he took turns with Sammy Tenizo selling tickets in a special booth.

The foreign team members had such behind-the-screens jobs as maintaining the bathrooms, running the projection room, cooking food and then ferrying it to us at the theater. It was going to be a long adventure—six shows a day for four days.

The first show began on schedule, but it was the many reel changeovers over the next four days that concerned us. Graeme and I had rehearsed the procedure beforehand, but we hadn't had a live audience watching.

At the first crucial changeover, the theater plunged into darkness, and our hands worked feverishly to get the second reel operating. The projection room's enormous 35mm projectors were constantly restricting our elbow room. In addition, we had no handy way to see the image on the screen because our 16mm projectors were shining through the peepholes that an operator of the 35mm monstrosities would use! The only holes left were near floor level, an extremely difficult position from which to focus!

Graeme had carefully watched the first reel down to the last frame on the celluloid. At that precise moment, he switched off the first projector and removed the precious special lens. Lens in hand, he stepped around all the projection room obstacles to thread the lens onto the second projector. He then set the reel in motion. All this time I was kneeling on the floor with my hand uncomfortably behind my back waiting for Graeme to grab my fingers and place them on the focusing mechanism of our projector. In this contorted position I was watching the blank screen, wondering how many seats our YWAM maintenance man would have to repair. It seemed like an eternity to me, but Graeme was actually moving quickly.

Now that the second reel was rolling, it was my job to do the focusing. My hand was sweaty, and my heart was in my mouth. I had brought movies into focus a hundred times, yet I couldn't seem to get it right this time. I was imagining fingers ripping at holes in the upholstery of the seats below. When I finally got off the floor and leaned against the bench at the back of the projection room, my heart was pounding wildly.

"That was a disaster!" I said. "How in the world can we do

twenty-three more changeovers during the next four days?" I babbled.

Graeme plucked nervously at his red sideburns as we talked. We were still in a state of high anxiety a full ten minutes later when an idea came to me.

"I know!" I said with a tinge of triumph now in my voice. "Why don't we show that slide about plunging the theater into darkness. That will give us more time while we do the changeover!"

A look of incredulity on Graeme's face stared back at me.

"That's exactly what I suggested to you."

Now it was my turn to be incredulous. Graeme and I were like brothers and discussed everything, but I couldn't remember his saying that. But it didn't matter.

"Then let's do it!" I replied, my heart now pounding with excitement. "That way we won't feel so pressured during each changeover!"

Bringing the slide projector into use required the assistance of a third person. Now three of us had to be in the projection room each time we changed reels. This demanded coordination and precise timing. The person taking the lens from one projector to the other always had to be careful not to trip over the cords, which could pull our valuable equipment crashing to the floor. If that ever happened, it would be the end of our showings. It was still nerve-racking, but the knowledge that the theater contained live people who needed Christ kept us motivated.

The Luna Theater often showed kung fu movies, and sure enough, kung fu fans filed into the theater the first day. Many were not impressed with our film and didn't hesitate to tell our Filipino staff. Others just showed their lack of interest on their faces. I tried to encourage our team. We could expect such a reaction at first. Don't worry about it. This is God's film, and the tide will change. But the comments by the kung fu fans still stung, especially with the disaster of our first changeover so fresh in my mind.

The second day brought a different kind of clientele, more serious-minded students. The word must have gotten out to the kung fu crowd to give us a wide berth. Even so, numbers were increasing, and we began hanging the "Standing Room Only" sign.

Comments now were positive and encouraging. The gospel theme and the message of sexual purity were getting through. We felt a strong sense of God at work. These people we loved were being touched by the Lord.

It was hard work, yet in our love for the Lord and for the students in the city, we enjoyed the challenge. We had staff at the theater from 9:30 each morning until 11:00 at night. The hours were long, and the jobs were not always easy. Bob Grierson, from South Africa, had a particularly difficult task cleaning the tiny bathrooms used by the crowds throughout the long days. Although starting times for the movies were posted, people walked into the theater at all times, adding to our workload. Despite this, Virgie, Fred, Flor, Rose, Helma, and Vangie—Filipinos from our staff and from our student center—cheerfully showed people to their seats hour after hour.

But if the hard work kept flowing, so did the inspiration, as crowds of students, assigned by their teachers to see the movie and then write a review, kept surging into the theater.

And thanks to our blindness slide, only three or four seats were torn up. Our maintenance man sewed them up with characteristic good humor.

At the end of four very busy and fulfilling days, almost 5,000 people had seen the movie during the twenty-four showings. Five thousand pesos—more than a laborer's annual income in 1977 and six times what they had expected—had been raised for the home for the blind.

We were happy—and exhausted. But since it was the spiritual results we wanted to preserve, we entered into two days of special prayer and fasting for the film's message to continue to impact lives. Response cards appeared in our post office box from those touched by the film, and our team members who visited these people reported they'd never done more exciting follow-up work. It was evident that in the darkness and quietness of that theater, these seekers—especially young women—had been deeply spoken to through the film's story of Carol's resisting sexual temptation and living completely for Christ.

Some who came to the Lord started attending our student center meetings. One young woman completed our Discipleship

Training School a few years later and then became a missionary to the island of Mindanao.

~ ~ ~ ~

After the euphoria of the *Two a Penny* showings subsided, I turned my thoughts toward the movie version of *The Cross and the Switchblade*, the best-selling book by David Wilkerson. The movie tells the true story of a country preacher's one-man mission among gang members in the concrete jungles of New York.

Philippine theaters had screened the film five years earlier when Margaret and I were in Europe. One day I noticed that the movie was back at a theater in Baguio. Since I'd never seen the film, I bought a ticket and watched it in an almost empty cinema.

I thought, *What would happen if we were to hire a theater and run the film in Baguio with our kind of promotion?* It would be easier to show than *Two a Penny*, since 35mm prints were available. I knew its rough-and-tumble action would also appeal to kung fu lovers, who had not been attracted to our showing of *Two a Penny*. But they needed the love of God, too.

I approached the distributor, a serious Chinese businesswoman named Mrs. Teh, who looked at me incredulously. "Don't you know that film has already shown five times in Baguio?"

"No, I didn't," I replied.

That didn't worry me, however. The *Two a Penny* showings had proven that by prayer and school promotions, we could fill the theater. Mrs. Teh's pessimistic attitude allowed us to book the film for the low rental fee of only 100 pesos (about $30 US).

We showed *The Cross and the Switchblade* just six weeks after *Two a Penny*, and once again, our work paid off, with good numbers in attendance. The showings coincided with Graeme and Mary's desire to start a Discipleship Training School, the first ever YWAM school in Asia. The movie provided a good introduction to the school, since the screenings gave our students opportunities for evangelism. The film also raised 2,000 pesos, which represented one student's fees for the five-month school.

Mrs. Teh was astonished when she heard how many people had

seen the film and warmly invited me to discuss film promotions over lunch at a Chinese restaurant. She could hardly contain her exuberance as she introduced me to her husband, who was also in the movie business.

"This is the man who took *The Cross and the Switchblade* to Baguio, where it had already shown many times, and yet thousands came to see it. And before that, his group screened a 16mm Billy Graham film to nearly 5,000 people!"

Mr. Teh smiled benignly. Although I was grateful for the recognition, I felt that what we had done was minuscule compared to the numbers in the Manila movie scene. There, a big movie might open simultaneously in forty theaters, screen as many as eight times a day, and still be showing in one or two theaters six weeks later!

Over many mouth-watering Chinese dishes, which included sweet and sour fish and smoked pork, and innumerable refills of tea, Mrs. Teh shared what was on her heart. She had recently imported *The Hiding Place* from World Wide Pictures, the film division of the Billy Graham Evangelistic Association. She related how, when it first showed in Manila, the movie opened in four theaters and was still showing in one theater three weeks later, quite an accomplishment for a Christian movie.

"But Ross, think what it could do with your kind of promotion. Could you and your team help me promote it throughout the rest of the Philippines?"

"I'll need to see it first," I replied.

"There's a small preview room nearby. Can you look at it now?"

Right away I saw potential in the Corrie ten Boom story of faith and forgiveness in Nazi-occupied Holland. The team swung into action, promoting the film in Baguio, where it opened in the very theater in which we had opposed *The Exorcist*. Our staff was back at the theater, not to protest, but this time to sell *The Hiding Place* books and t-shirts. We thrilled at the crowds pouring in for five daily showings to watch an uplifting Christian movie.

The standing-room-only crowds caused the theater to regret its decision to limit the film to just one week, the typical run of a movie in Baguio. Fortunately, another theater picked the film up and showed it for an additional ten days, making the length of the Baguio showings a near record-breaking two and a half weeks!

A delighted Mrs. Teh then shared with us her plans for nation-wide showings of *The Hiding Place*. She began flying me throughout the country to contact leaders at key high schools and colleges who would assign their students to watch the movie as part of their curriculum. I contacted TV and radio stations, which often interviewed me on the spot.

My work paved the way for our teams, who sailed from city to city with boxes of books, t-shirts, and handouts. Our team members seized any opportunity to promote the film on radio or by speaking at civic clubs. They also did the all-important work of contacting head teachers in both public and Catholic schools. We provided each teacher with comprehensive notes that we had written so they could lead their students in discussions on the spiritual message of the movie. In this way we were loving the country's youth and affecting them in a positive way.

Spurred on by all this activity, Mrs. Teh imported two 35mm prints of *Two a Penny*. Things had been going well. In just a couple of years we had gone from showing one 16mm *sine* with a borrowed projector in Baguio to promoting proper cinema movies that showed throughout the Philippines to standing-room-only crowds.

We were now influencing hundreds of thousands by film, radio, and TV. Even more thrilling were the activities we engaged in behind the scenes, such as speaking at civic clubs, over the air, or in the schools. We were often in classrooms teaching students who had seen the movie and were now asking thoughtful questions. It was not just YWAMers who did the spiritual work. In the University of the Philippines—the nation's most prestigious university—I watched a Christian student openly lead a friend to Christ in the classroom where I had just been speaking.

Through our work we were rubbing shoulders with business people, educators, church and civic leaders, and prominent members of the media and the movie industry. In city after city we approached newspapers with articles we had written, some not even related to our movies; virtually every article was published.

When we returned to Baguio, the film *Jesus of Nazareth* was showing at the Pines Theater, which had declined *The Omen* as a result of our protest. We immediately threw our support behind the movie, which ran for over two weeks!

Then *Jesus of Nazareth* opened in Iligan, a city on Mindanao near a heavily populated Muslim region. One of our teams was already in the area, and the members needed no prompting to swing into action. They approached a radio station and were granted a one-hour interview. On the air with them was a local Christian, who spoke boldly about the Son of God in a local dialect used almost exclusively by Muslims.

We were on a roll!

But we didn't know what lay just around the corner...

Faith That Works By Love

During that time, it was relatively easy for me to rise to the challenge of the hard work before me. I loved the Philippines and her people. There have been other times, however, when it's been difficult for me to rise in faith and believe that God will impact a situation, not because I was unsure of what God's overall will was, based on His character, but I must admit, because of my own apathy and lack of love.

In the Bible, Jonah had a similar problem. He did not want to preach in Nineveh. He didn't like the people and didn't want them saved (Jonah 1:1-3; 3:1-4:3). With me, it wasn't necessarily that I didn't like some people; I just didn't like them enough. The apostle Paul hesitated to do certain things, but he spoke of Christ's love compelling him (2 Cor. 5:14).

What happens when we don't feel that surge of love? By faith we sometimes have to tell ourselves, "This is the will of God, so I will do it." In my experience, if I perform an *action* of love towards someone I have little feeling for, the *emotions* follow later. This is merely the outworking of Jesus' exhortation, "Do good to them that hate you" (Matt. 5:44, KJV). Jesus didn't say to *feel* love; He told us to *do* love.

In a coming chapter we will see that our faith can even be motivated by pride and vainglory. Scripturally, our love for others should motivate us. Galatians 5:6 read: "The only thing that counts is faith expressing itself through love." If not rooted in care for God's glory and concern for others, our faith is empty ritual.

By faith all things are possible, but with love all things are easier.

It took a lot of hard work preparing for those four days in the Luna Theater that launched the team into its theater ministry. In fact, the work became even harder and required longer hours once the film got rolling. As the teams carried on with the film ministry, their workload grew. But with love in their hearts, they not only survived the task but also reveled in it and rejoiced day after day as God showed His love to many people.

Receiving a word from God to embark on a course of action does not mean that the devil will let us alone or that our project will automatically succeed. The Bible teaches that we **will** face opposition when we step out in faith and at times there will be fierce battles to wage.

The book of Joshua declares it was God's will for the children of Israel to take Canaan, but enemy attacks and temptations sometimes left the Israelites discouraged, subdued, and in danger of not possessing their inheritance. However, in our walk of faith today, we need not be defeated, because God has given us weapons of spiritual warfare with which to resist Satan (Eph. 6:11-17).

In the Philippines, the enemy used numerous devices to try to thwart our God-given ministry promoting Christian movies. For a long while everything had been going well. But then the battles began...

CHAPTER SEVEN

Faith and Spiritual Warfare

If we thought Satan would leave our movie ministry unopposed, we were being naive. It was critical that we not let up in our prayers. Once *The Hiding Place* had played in Manila, Cebu, Davao, and Baguio, we started encountering difficulties for future bookings. A major point of contention was the common practice of showing two films as a double feature. We often had a war on our hands over what the second film should be.

Mrs. Teh was well-known as a distributor of the violent kung fu movies that are highly popular with many young Filipino males. Often she'd call me from Manila to plead her case: "Ross, this time we really *must* show a kung fu movie as the double!" She knew our position on this: *The Hiding Place* and a kung fu movie did not go together. One preached forgiveness, the other violence and revenge.

"In that case," I'd reply with as much grace as I could muster, "we will have to ask our team to stop promoting the showings."

We went through this drama more than once. Mrs. Teh knew that without our promotion, the movie would flop. Eventually, she and the theater manager would consent to *The Cross and the Switchblade* as the second film.

From Dagupan, a small city near Baguio, team leader Sammy Tenizo called in with glowing reports on the film crowds there.

"Lots of students are entering the theater," he cheerfully told me each day.

But every night, Mrs. Teh called from Manila to say, "Ross! The Dagupan showings are doing poorly!"

I couldn't figure out what was happening.

We eventually learned that the theater manager was so angry about having to show *The Cross and the Switchblade* rather than a kung fu *sine* that he schemed with a city official to cheat Mrs. Teh out of her rightful share of the ticket sales. But that wasn't all. The projectionist deliberately mixed up the order of the five reels of *The Cross and the Switchblade*, seriously reducing the impact of the film.

Such opposition wasn't restricted to one city. In nearby San Fernando, La Union, someone started a bonfire in a vacant lot beside the theater showing *The Hiding Place*. The air-conditioning ducts sucked in the smoke, leading to panic inside. Thinking the building was on fire, the patrons fled and did not return.

Meanwhile, Mrs. Teh told me that a theater in yet another city refused to pay her for our packed-out showings of *The Hiding Place*. Despite her protests to the Philippine Association of Motion Picture Business, she never received a penny.

We'd experienced earlier attacks as well, but a huge volume of prayer had shielded us against them. I recalled a couple of instances related to our original *Two a Penny* showings in Baguio. One night I had left the Luna Theater, but when I reached the parking lot I felt a strange urge to return to the theater. I stood for a moment with my hand on the jeep's door handle before deciding to go back. I retraced my steps all the way up the stairs to the projection room and found the projectionist merrily writing a letter, oblivious to the fact that a bulb had blown and a standing-room-only crowd was watching an inky black screen.

The other instance occurred prior to the showings. A huge typhoon was predicted to hit us just before those four eventful days. We knew it had the potential for toppling trees, ripping down power lines, closing schools, and seriously affecting attendance. But in response to prayer, it veered off course. When it eventually hit Taiwan, the Taiwanese called it their worst ever.

Those episodes demonstrated to me that the prayers of God's people were effective. The opposition we experienced in Dagupan, San Fernando, and elsewhere now revealed the need for us to step up our prayer support.

Once *The Hiding Place* completed its circuit, our teams returned to concentrate on the student center work in Baguio and to be involved in evangelism throughout the country. In 1979, Graeme and his wife Mary left Baguio to set up a YWAM center in Davao. Later in the year I began to have stirrings about continuation of the film ministry, this time in Manila, where we had never before promoted films. I had sensed intensified enemy opposition to what we had done with movies in the provincial centers and wondered how it would go in Manila, the mecca of the Philippine movie industry.

In Manila's student belt, home to a half million students in cramped boarding houses, dozens of theaters and schools dotted the dreary asphalt landscape. Against this background, huge colorful billboards coaxed students into the theaters daily. In the 1970's, it was estimated that each week the equivalent of half of Manila's people—then 10 million—sought relief from the city's relentless heat, noise, and smog in air-conditioned theaters.

My goal for Manila was to book showings of the Billy Graham film *Time to Run*. For two years, the city's powerful booking agents had refused Mrs. Teh's pleas to show the movie. The plot centers on a workaholic father who neglects both his wife and his college-age son. Animosity builds to a level where the youth runs away. The family is later reconciled, but only after the son responds to the gospel at a Billy Graham crusade.

Despite its positive message, *Time to Run* left the Manila film bookers cold. With no bedroom scenes and no violence, not even a fist fight, none of them wanted to show it. The film appeared dead. But I believed that God had a strategy to get it shown in Manila. I knew it would take lots of hard work and all the components of spiritual warfare—hearing from God, persistent obedience to His direction, and faith in His character—but I was committed to getting the film shown. *People will hear the gospel this way,* I reasoned. *That's what counts!*

Every week for the next two months, I said goodbye to Margaret and our growing family (we now had three young sons, Mark, Stuart, and Warren) and took the six-hour bus ride from Baguio to Manila. I'd spend up to four days at a time working on getting *Time to Run* to screen in the Philippine capital.

My strategy was to contact as many school heads and counselors as possible and invite them to special preview showings of the film. After that, the plan was to ask them to write letters to the film industry requesting that the *sine* be shown. I hoped their letters would persuade Mrs. Teh's bookers to change their mind. I asked my friends at Chi Alpha Christian Student Center for contacts among teachers they knew, but usually I hit the schools with no contacts at all. Meeting up with busy school leaders was sometimes the hard part.

A few days of hit-or-miss film promoting in downtown Manila's oppressive humidity, congestion, and pollution convinced me of the need for more prayer in this battle, and each week when I returned to Baguio I asked the other team members for their intercession. I soon became very aware of tangible answers to those prayers.

One day as I was lunching at a crowded student-belt restaurant, I was struck by a sudden thought: *Go back to St. Beda High School right now.* I had already been there that morning to invite a school counselor to a preview for teachers at 2 p.m., but he hadn't been in. So why go back now? Surely no one would be in the office at lunchtime.

Go back to St. Beda High School right now. The same gentle but firm urging nudged me again. I tried to brush it off, but the impression wouldn't go away. Quickly I scooped the rest of my lunch into my mouth, drained the last of my soft drink, and headed for St. Beda High School.

During my morning visit, the receptionist at the large Catholic school had told me to come back much later in the day. I now felt stupid trying to explain to her why I had come back hours too soon.

"I'll just wait here in the hope that he will return earlier than expected," I said, feeling embarrassed. Inwardly, I sighed. *You really need a lot of humility to operate in faith.*

Suddenly the very man I was looking for walked in. He seemed completely unruffled to find me waiting, and he warmly heard me out. I then plunged in with what was uppermost on my mind.

"There's actually a preview scheduled in an hour," I said half eagerly, half hesitantly. "It's just a few blocks away."

"I have a class at that time," he replied thoughtfully, "but let me see what I can do." I left his office prayerful and hopeful he could make it.

An hour later he joined the other teachers who had already assembled in the preview room. He even brought the school principal. It was his turn to be apologetic.

"I hope you don't mind," he said.

Mind? This was an answer to prayer!

After the movie, I gave my pitch about the difficulty we'd had in getting a play date for *Time to Run.*

"Could you each possibly write a letter encouraging this theater to book the movie?" I asked. "And better still, would you each promise to assign your students to attend the showings? That will make all the difference. Please write your letter on your school stationary, and I'll come around and pick them up."

The prayers of God's people kept being answered. One night at the Chi Alpha Student Center, someone approached me with the name of the head teacher of a nearby high school, a Mr. Narag. Despite all my efforts over several days, I just couldn't contact him. One evening not long before dusk, as I was about to quit for the day, and inner urge spoke within. *Go back to Mr. Narag's school now.* It didn't make any sense! It was already 6 p.m., and no head teacher would be in his office at this late hour. But when you are engaged in spiritual warfare, it is important to obey any prompting of the Holy Spirit. I stood deep in thought for a moment.

For years, YWAM had rented an apartment near the Manila student belt that we used for housing outreach teams and staff when in Manila. I was using it as my headquarters on this present campaign, and I was looking forward to washing off Manila's grime and smog and flopping onto a bed. Concluding that this inner urge could not be God after all, I began walking towards a waiting jeep. But the prompting persisted. I hesitated again. I really was looking forward to a shower!

Finally, I let the jeep take off without me and slowly turned to walk the short distance back to the school, my briefcase feeling heavier than ever. Once inside the building, I was amazed at the number of people walking in the corridor. Heading in the direction of the school offices, I suddenly felt that inner voice again. *Speak to that man!* I had nothing to lose, so I approached the man walking towards me.

"Excuse me, but could you tell me where I can find Mr. Narag?"

I felt a little self-conscious. Surely he would not be around at this time. But I didn't have to be hesitant.

"I'm Mr. Narag!" he replied.

❧ ❧ ❧ ❧

I was to learn that Mr. Narag's high school was one of the city's largest. During the next preview of the film, Mr. Narag was so impressed with its message that he wrote to say that he'd make it mandatory for 2,000 students to see it! A commitment like that was like pure gold in influencing the bookers!

After the two previews, I began collecting the letters I'd requested. School leaders told me that they'd support *Time to Run* because their students were so needy in the area of morals and family life. The head counselor of St. Beda told me how much he had enjoyed the movie as well as the four-page teacher's guide I had written.

"If the film shows, I'll turn your teacher's guide into an exam once my students have seen the movie!"

By October 2, I had enough letters to take to the booker recommended by Mrs. Teh. Before leaving, I asked the staff in Baguio to remember me in specific intercession. Special requests for prayer were telexed off to YWAM centers abroad.

When I met with the booker, he was immediately impressed with all the letters I'd collected.

"What a great idea! I'd like to see this film immediately."

Within hours, I sat between the booker and the manager of a student belt theater watching the movie in a tiny preview room. Judging by their dour expressions, I could tell that the film left them unmoved.

I could only resort to prayer. The men I was appealing to could easily signal that they'd seen enough after just one 20-minute reel and dismiss the whole idea. I therefore prayed through as much as the movie as possible. However, I was afraid that if the men seated next to me were to see me with my head bowed and my hands gesturing they would think I was nuts. I thus took advantage of the night scenes of the film to implore God fervently and rebuke Satan from influencing these two men. At the end of the film, I had the distinct feeling that the men would not have watched the entire film had I not been there interceding and making comments from time to time. I waited for some sign of their thinking.

"I'll be contacting Mrs. Teh," is all I got.

When I asked her the next day, Mrs. Teh said she'd heard nothing.

"In this business, Ross, you have to give a bribe."

"Don't you dare!" I shot back.

I had now been in the Philippines eight years and was very aware of the cultural acceptance of bribery. But I had conducted my personal affairs and those of the mission with the belief that we shouldn't yield to this practice. The apostle Paul's example in Acts 24:26 and many other Scriptures confirmed this to me even though there were consequences for taking this stand. We once waited six months to clear a shipment through customs.

"God's work has to be done in God's way," I continued.

Mrs. Teh smiled but said no more. She then reached for the work she'd received from a commercial artist to advertise the film. I couldn't believe my eyes. She held up a painting of Jeff, the movie's main character, with his girlfriend in a scene that didn't even appear in the film. The picture was designed to created the impression that this was a romantic movie.

I was so appalled that I said I'd withdraw from the promotion of the film if she used that artwork. A visitor in her office who was also involved in the movie business looked at me as if I were from another planet! Both he and Mrs. Teh could see nothing to object to.

What do I do know?

With the thought that the booker wouldn't budge without a bribe and the disappointment of the advertising poster weighing heavily on my heart, I walked slowly down the stairs into Manila's smog. Even though the sun had set, it was still hot and humid.

It seemed as though all my backbreaking work had been futile. My mind counted up all the weeks I had been absent from Margaret, our three boys, and beautiful, green Baguio with its fresh mountain air. As I threaded my way in the darkened streets through the heavy pedestrian traffic to a preaching appointment, I felt my spirit sinking to the lowest point in my life of faith yet. *If someone were to jump from the shadows and attack me right now, I just wouldn't care!*

❧ ❧ ❧ ❧

I dragged myself from my self-pity trip long enough to preach as scheduled at the Chi Alpha Student Center. Many at the meeting were friends, and they enjoyed what I had to say. At the end of the service, it was ironic that I felt so fine, but it was even more ironic that I had chosen the topic of faith to speak about.

After three days, there was still no word from the booker. Mrs. Teh suggested that I see his boss, but she first warned me that he was the man who had initially rejected the film. This didn't stop me. It just meant that we had to pray all the harder against the enemy's efforts to block the film.

I was convinced that God wanted this movie shown and the gospel preached through it. I prayed about the timing of my visit. So much hinged on the outcome of this meeting that I wanted to be absolutely sure I had the Lord's leading.

At the hour I felt God had said, I climbed the stairs to the tiny office and found myself facing a thin-faced, bespectacled business-man. I cleared my throat, and the man peered from the papers and folders piled untidily on his desk. I quickly explained the purpose of my visit and told him about the support we had from local schools. When I had finished, he looked at me as if I had presented him with a very viable business proposition. I had come braced for a battle, so I was surprised when he started checking his schedule.

"Okay, we'll show that film starting October 19."

I could hardly believe it! I thanked him and bounded down the stairs two at a time. The whole incident had taken about four minutes flat!

I knew it wasn't the greatest date, but I had suggested October 19 because it would be during semester break. I figured the movie czar would let our film show at that time because many college students would be out of town, and he wouldn't want to use that time for any blockbuster movies. Yet it would still be a fair enough time, since it was usually the students from high school, not college students, that teachers assigned to see our movies. And high schools didn't close for the semester break!

I returned to Baguio in high spirits and quickly began preparing the staff for our first ever showings in Manila. After all we'd been through, I should have realized that the devil wasn't going to give in that easily. But I didn't think much of it until the phone rang a few days later. It was Mrs. Teh.

"Ross!" she said in her brisk manner. "I've been advised by the booker that *Time to Run* will not definitely start on October 19."

"Why not?" I replied, dumbfounded.

"Because they have told me we must be prepared to start screening at any time between October 14 and 19!

"And Ross!" she added for emphasis. "If not enough people see the movie the first day, the theater will pull it!"

I groaned as I hung up the phone. Having no firm opening date would be horrible even for a secular distributor with a strong film. It allowed no time for proper advertising. The schools were dependent on having an exact date, especially since it would be around exam time. The whole idea was disastrous!

But worse was the threat of the movie's being pulled after only one day before everyone would have a chance to see it. I had never heard of such an arrangement.

We had no choice but to pray and make the best of it. In early October, our eight-member team loaded bags and boxes into our faithful 13-seater jeepney and headed for Manila. During the film's run, we'd all be staying together at our YWAM apartment near the theater district.

We had been informed that *Time to Run* would show in one

other theater across town in the populous area of Cubao. That was a mixed blessing. We were delighted to have another location, but I had done little promotion in the area. We'd have a lot of work to do to make the Cubao showings a success.

After breakfast the next morning in Manila, we pulled together for our plan of attack.

It was a thrill to be closely working with a team again. Most of them were converts from YWAM's years in the Philippines—Rey and Helen from Davao; Richie from the Baguio *Two a Penny* adventure and Conchita and Arlene from our student center work. Bob from South Africa, Jackie from Switzerland and Joan from Australia filled out the hard-working group.

Each day we asked the Lord to help us prepare for the start of the showings, still not certain when it would be sprung upon us. It was really nerve-racking. We particularly appealed to friendly school heads to be ready to send their students to the cinema the very first day the movie began to show.

In prayer one day, I sensed that the mystery date would be October 16. I thought of the repercussions of announcing it to all the schools and then perhaps discovering I was wrong. I just couldn't bring myself to make any pronouncements.

We continued to work hard. Even our jeep was pressed into service promoting the film by lugging huge signs strapped to either side of the vehicle as it traveled several times to Cubao and back.

When the call came from Mrs. Teh, I shouldn't have been surprised at the opening date. It was to be the next day, Tuesday, October 16! Tuesday was an unheard of day for a new film to open, as Manila theaters used Thursday or Friday as their normal changeover day. We made many calls that day to get the word out! I began to wistfully think of what might have happened if I'd paid closer attention to the impression I'd had earlier. God had been faithful to speak. I regretted I had not been faithful to respond. Now things were going to be more difficult!

We split our group in two so that each theater would have team members on hand to pass out our specially written handouts or sell our literature and *Time to Run* T-shirts. These T-shirts were important, since once sold, they went everywhere on people's backs advertising the film.

Tuesday dawned, and the teams were set in place at both theaters. I continued to call head teachers and visit schools. It was imperative that many students enter the theater this first day. The excitement I felt left me with little time to fret, but I tried my best to gauge how well the showings were going. At day's end, I was relieved to hear that both theaters would carry the film the next day.

Now the ball was rolling! If we could just keep enough people coming, we might hang in through the weekend when crowds were always much better. Wednesday attendance continued strong, but Thursday—the day when new films opened in other theaters—was a disaster. Attendance dropped to less that half the levels of the previous two days. The handwriting was on the wall. I could see us losing both theaters.

We were informed that the Cubao showings would be discontinued, but mercifully the showings at the theater in the student belt would continue. What a relief! But I deeply grieved the loss of the Cubao showings, since over the weekend, I knew that the movie would have appealed to many families in Cubao. What might have happened if I'd listened more carefully to that urge concerning the opening day?

The two teams now joined forces, and with the extra help came an idea suggested by the movie itself. At the end of the film, Billy Graham exhorts viewers to leave their theater seats and "come to the front where counselors are available to talk to you."

In the States, the movie had been intended to be shown in a rented theater, where Christians were at liberty to run the show as they pleased and thus have altar calls. Over the past two days, fellow team members had approached me about their going to the front of the theater in the event people wanted to talk.

"But these showings are strictly a commercial enterprise arranged between Mrs. Teh and the theater," I replied.

Even with my opportunistic tendencies, I didn't think we had this liberty. But with more team members in one place now and the theater still now attracting big crowds, I thought we could discreetly give it a go. Rey was particularly keen to try.

It worked the very first time! At almost every one of the seven showings that first day, someone came to talk to Rey at one side of the theater or to Joan at the other. I was half expecting the theater manager to protest, but he said nothing.

On each of the succeeding days, Rey followed this procedure with the same results. Meanwhile, outside the theater, other team members sold dozens of *Time to Run* T-shirts and copies of Billy Graham's paperback *How to Be Born Again.*

Moviegoers stopped to ask questions or to even receive counsel from our team members as they distributed the handouts. The whole theater had become a chapel, with a small room near the stage area becoming the "holy of holies," where Rey would direct people who had responded to the appeal given by Dr. Graham.

For a week, Rey stood at the front of the theater and led seekers into that small room with its bare floor and wooden table and chairs. After spending the next two hours with them, he had just enough time for a quick cola or some *pan de sal* bread before starting the process all over again. People were constantly coming to the Lord through the thoroughness of Rey's patient counseling. What a long way Rey had come from his preconversion days in Davao!

The numbers coming to the Lord sent me rejoicing as I drove the jeep around the city visiting more schools to drum up more trade. I was proud of the entire team. The members all fulfilled their roles perfectly as they worked at the theater, delivered promotional literature, or helped me call the schools. Often we put in fourteen-hour days. Each night about 11 p.m. we would regroup at the apartment and share a meal together, all the while rejoicing and praising God over the current day's story.

After ten days, the theater management declared they were ending the film's run. It was hard not to be disappointed, but the closing gave us the opportunity to concentrate on follow-up. Additionally, *Time to Run* would at last be free to be shown in other parts of the country. During the Manila showings, Mrs. Teh had told us that a theater owner from the city of Bacolod had seen the film at one of our screenings and had booked it into his theater. She wanted to fly me down to the sugar-growing island of Negros in the center of the Philippines to encourage the showings. I quickly accepted her invitation.

It was good to be out in the province again, and I enjoyed the challenge of approaching the Bacolod media to promote the film. In those few days, I was granted four radio interviews and one on TV. Even more enjoyable was the preview for twenty-five high school teachers that I managed to arrange with the help of a missionary friend who had agreed to help Mrs. Teh with the Bacolod showings.

Back in Manila, the others continued to follow up those who had come to Christ.

The screening of *Time to Run* in Manila represented the most challenging spiritual warfare I was involved in with the films. It also realized the greatest spiritual results. This is quite understandable, for in my view, spiritual warfare and greater spiritual results go together.

Spiritual Warfare

I see a parallel between Joshua's battles in Canaan and the spiritual battles we waged with our Christian films. Joshua had received a mandate from God to take the nations of the promised land, just as the Lord commissioned us to show Christian movies. But just because a thing is the will of God doesn't mean it will automatically come to pass. In the early chapters of the book of Joshua, Israel had a mixture of successes and setbacks before victory, despite the mandate to take the land. Satan tried many ways to resist Israel's advances.

During the time of Christ's earthly ministry, Satan used various means to oppose Jesus. His armory included the jealousy of the Pharisees, tricky questions from religious legalists, the yelling of demons, storms on the lake, and even the unfaithfulness of some of Jesus' own followers. He was tempted in all points, as are we (Heb. 4:15).

It is to be expected that once we receive guidance from God to attempt something useful for His kingdom we will experience opposition. Because the film industry is enemy-occupied territory, we should have been prepared for the struggles we encountered.

In recent times as I've been more diligently interceding, I've observed increased blessing on this ministry. But I've also noticed an increase in spiritual opposition. How are we to respond to this opposition?

If the episodes of Joshua in Canaan and the life of Jesus teach us anything, they instruct us that we must always be spiritually alert. Ephesians 6:18 exhorts us to pray at all times in the Spirit with all prayer and petition for one another. I've noticed that when weird things happen against my ministry and I recruit special prayer, those bizarre things—such as a disturbed night, mysterious physical pains, or computer equipment problems—start to abate.

Because prayer cuts off Satan's attacks, the enemy will seek to obstruct those who pray. Someone who intercedes for me two mornings a week once said she has noticed repeatedly that those two mornings get "invaded" either by children falling sick or workmen turning up unexpectedly. She has discovered that she must wage spiritual warfare in advance to protect those mornings from disruption. Satan knows what blunts his attacks: intercession waged in the Spirit with the right motivation. I'm convinced that had we not prayed and recruited prayer from around the world, our film ministry would have accomplished little.

I am in total awe of the concept of Christians waging spiritual warfare through obedience and intercession because of the results that I continually see. When God has all the power in the world, you wouldn't think that He needed to use our cooperation and fervent prayers to accomplish His purposes. But that is the way He has chosen. Moses' time of intercession to save the children of Israel from their impending destruction is a powerful illustration of this (Ex. 32:7-14; Ps. 106:21-23).

When Adam and Eve first yielded to Satan, they gave him spiritual rights to operate on this planet. Every time anyone sins today, it gives the devil another opportunity to impact the world for evil. That is what is meant by "do not give the devil a foothold" (Eph. 4:27).

By the same token, whenever we obey God and resist the devil, we take back territory for the Lord. As the scripture plainly reveals, "Submit yourselves to God, resist the devil and he will flee from you" (James 4:7).

It has been my experience that for us to see our faith goals realized, God requires us to wage a spiritual battle. That warfare embodies not just prayer, however. It involves first our hearing from

God and then persevering in both obedience and *fervent* prayer. If we give up any part, we risk losing what God has given us to achieve by faith.

*Early in our walk of faith, we all have to face the challenge that what counts is not **what** we do for God but **why** we do it. Obviously, a loving, friendly God wants our service because we are devoted to Him. Our Christian work may not be perfect, but our motivation must be. "Create in me a pure heart, O God" (Ps. 51:10).*

Of all the reasons why stepping out in faith may not have worked for some, this is the subtlest. But it is even more subtle when you start out with a pure motive and end up with a tainted one.

Chapter Eight

Check Your Motives!

The well-traveled letter in my hand bore a distinctive stamp that could only be from India. The return address revealed that the letter was from a YWAM friend now living in Madras. As I tore open the letter, I fondly recalled the time Margaret and I had spent teaching on the Indian subcontinent the year after our marriage.

That was so long ago and far away now. Here we were, after seventeen years in missions—most of them in the Philippines—taking some time off to study at YWAM's University of the Nations in Kona, Hawaii. Our time in the classes was refreshing, but the friendships we'd left behind and their needs were always on our minds.

The letter in my hand turned my thoughts back to India. It was an invitation to speak for a week at a school of evangelism starting in Madras early the following year of 1984. I wanted to accept immediately, but I knew that no YWAM school in India could afford to cover my roundtrip airfare. My traveling expenses would have to be provided by my own faith in God! I clearly needed a word from Him on this because I had no finances of my own for such a trip.

I mused on the prospects of a trip for several weeks before setting aside a special time to seek the Lord in the prayer room at the university. I spent unhurried time before the Lord, and in due course a word came to my heart. *Accept this invitation.*

"OK, Lord. But I am now asking you for the large amount that will be needed for the airfare."

We were still getting used to the high cost of living in Hawaii which, after years in the Philippines, seemed astronomical. Soon after arrival in Hawaii, we took Mark, aged ten, and Stuart, aged seven, to a doctor who charged us seventy dollars just to tell us they had a virus. Such a visit in Baguio would have cost two or three dollars!

The next day I climbed the stairs to the prayer room to again pray about the money I would need before leaving. But that day, God quickened a verse that read, "Take no gold, or silver, or copper in your belts." Instinctively I knew what God was saying to me. *The money would not come in before I left. Some would be given to me as I traveled.*

On the third day, He revealed that even though this trip was in His will, it wouldn't be easy. It was the same message I'd learned through our film showings: I'd reach my goal only by pressing in spiritually against the powers of darkness.

I cabled Madras to expect me on February 11, 1984. Since I planned to spend a week in the Philippines and a couple of days in Thailand en route to India, I figured I'd need to leave Kona on the night of January 30.

But by January 29, I had only $50 for the trip with a promise of another $80. With no other finances to lean on, the outlook seemed to get bleaker by the hour. On the afternoon of my departure date, the situation remained unchanged. By now I had sent word to the Philippines and Thailand about my arrival times as well.

I had also made arrangements with a Honolulu travel agent to have a one-way ticket to Manila sent to meet my flight from Kona. The ticket would be hand carried to the airport by a YWAMer whom I knew. I was to hand him the $350 to pay the travel agent.

Time was running out, but it still felt like I was breaking one of the Ten Commandments to let anyone know about my financial needs, unless they asked, of course. As I showered, I calculated the amount I still needed.

Despite the outward circumstances, I knew the situation was not hopeless for God. Since He'd told me to make this trip, He would provide as long as I was obeying Him with the right motivation. Just the day before, I had preached in a local church, and the pastor said he'd be giving me an honorarium. Of course, he didn't know my need, and I didn't know how much the honorarium would be. Nor did I know whether it would even reach me before my scheduled departure time.

After showering, I heard a knock at the door. There, to my great delight, stood the pastor, who handed me a check that amounted to what I still needed for a one-way ticket to Manila and left me with a few dollars to spare. But I still would have no ticket beyond the Philippines, either to proceed to India or to return to Hawaii.

I flew off that night, again amazed at God's incredible timing. I wondered about all the money I still needed but remembered the word the God had given me in the prayer room: He would provide as I traveled. He had spoken. That was the main thing.

At the Honolulu airport, I was met by a woman who earlier had asked me to carry a carton of milk powder and some money to an orphanage in Manila. When she finished her instructions, she added with a broad smile, "I had an extra $80, so I prayed about what I should do with it. I feel it's for you."

She had no way of knowing how close to the wire I was traveling!

Arriving in the Philippines, the YWAM Filipino staff gave me a royal welcome. It was a delight to renew fellowship with several people I had ministered with over the years. It was a particular joy to see Mike and Janice Shelling who had recently returned to the Philippines from Minnesota. They were still planning to fulfill Mike's long-term plan to reach mountain people north of Baguio. It felt so good to chat about old times and future plans.

The days slipped by in long and cheerful conversations with my Filipino friends in both Manila and Baguio. Many pressed precious, hard-earned pesos into my hand as we parted. I was genuinely moved by their love and generosity. Nonetheless, those pesos amounted to about $50, far below the amount I needed for a one-way airfare to Bangkok. I had to work at not worrying about my plight.

On a whim I had brought with me an expired Manila-to-Bangkok ticket on the off chance that someone at Philippine Airlines night extend it for me. The chances were slim, as the ticket was now more than two years old. They became even slimmer when I learned that my chief contact at the airline office had been transferred out of the country. But when my departure day arrived, I flew to Thailand on that very two-year-old ticket!

I spent the next day in steamy downtown Bangkok, wandering through the noisy streets, looking for a ticket to India. All I had was just $30. Once again I needed a miracle.

I prayed and thought as I walked. What a crazy situation this would be to try to explain. Here I was in Bangkok, with not enough money to continue on to India, or to return home, even if I wanted to.

"Of course, Lord, I know you could send an angel with a ticket or even translate me to India without a plane. I am simply obeying what you've told me to do. I am not mad at you, God!"

Since that time on the floor as a 19-year-old, I had been in jams like this many, many times. But always the memory of that experience came to my assistance. I pressed into the Lord as I walked around the travel agency area of Bangkok, making sure I wasn't letting any feeling of poor me creep in. Boy, did I pray!

I didn't recognize it then, but I was letting another attitude, just as bad as self-pity, slip in. I began thinking of how embarrassing it would be if I were to end up stuck in Bangkok. I began to pray even harder.

In terms of getting a ticket to India, however, it made no difference. I still returned that night to the house where I was staying empty-handed. *People from the YWAM Madras base will be expecting my arrival tomorrow,* I reminded myself. And here I am, stuck in Thailand with no money. The only positive thing I'd heard so far was that the best flight to India didn't leave until tomorrow evening. Although it would mean a midnight arrival in India, I would still have all day Sunday to rest up before a week of speaking each morning and evening. And there was still time for God to provide for the trip!

I had told no one of my needs.

That night I took part in a time of praise and worship with fellow missionary volunteers. It was then that I heard God speak. During worship time, God reminded me that I had been pressing in that day for the ticket. It was true. I really had.

But the reason has not been so that Christ will be formed in East Indians, the Lord seemed to say to my heart. It was supposed to be. I was to speak on the subject of evangelism.

The reason you've been pressing in to Me, He continued, *has been so that you wouldn't look like a big fool stranded here in Thailand.*

The truth of His comment immediately stung my heart.

"Oh, Lord, You're so right!" I responded. "Please forgive my pride."

How subtly my pure motivation had changed to a self-centered one! After repenting, I began to pray that Jesus would use my visit to India to help form His character within the students I would be teaching. I had barely finished praying when the bespectacled young man sitting beside me gently nudged me. Because the group was still worshiping, he whispered to me, "How much money do you need to buy a ticket to India?"

I whispered back the amount. That was the end of the conversation. The praise meeting continued.

Next morning this same young man with glasses came down the stairs where I was staying and greeted me. After conversing for a while, he said, "You know, God spoke to me last night during the worship time to buy you a round-trip ticket from here to India. But I waited until now to be really sure. After breakfast," he continued, "I'll take you downtown and pick up a ticket from my travel agent."

That evening I was on an AirLanka plane. Despite the very short connection time between flights in Sri Lanka, not only did I make the connection, but my luggage did, too. Smiling Indian YWAM faces were there to meet me as I arrived at the Madras airport right on schedule. As my taxi sped past people, bikes, and oxcarts, even at this late hour, I knew I was back in India!

Significantly, God gave me a series of messages quite different from the ones I had prepared. I gave messages on evangelism at night, but during the day, I presented a new series on interpersonal relationships in the Third World that reflected both my studies in

Hawaii and my years in Asia. The classes were so well received that I offered to speak on Saturday, too. Those voluntary morning and evening classes were attended by everyone!

A large group stayed up until midnight on my last night to bid me farewell before I left for the flight that would take me back to Thailand. God provided some of the money for the flight back to Hawaii in India itself. The rest came in Thailand, where I spent a week ministering en route back home.

Postscript

Four months later, I was back in India, trusting God for finances while speaking in yet another school. Several years later I took a team of fourteen to Madras from Kona. For years after that trip, seven continued to work in India. Even today, six years later, nine of the original group are scattered around the world in full-time Christian service.

That step-by step trip to Madras in 1984 underscores a principle I had seen earlier through other trips. A victory gained through a baptism of fire in the beginning paves the way for greater things to come.

Check Your Motives

The main scriptural lesson of my experience in Bangkok was that God requires us to serve Him with a pure heart. God also showed me that if my *motives* aren't right, He will gently correct me if I'll listen and obey.

Just because we start out with pure motives doesn't mean we'll always continue with them. I had left for India in simple obedience to God, but by the time I had reached Bangkok, pride had crept in. That's why it's so important to always be listening to the Lord. We may not like it when He speaks a word of correction to us, but let us be happy that He does. God doesn't speak to the spiritually dead.

God is not restricted to crises such as mine to test our attitudes. Several months ago I was shocked to uncover my own self-centered motives in even wanting to pray for revival in our present work. If we're getting ready to launch out in faith, let's first ask ourselves some hard questions. Do we really want this faith project to flourish for God's glory? Or do we have hidden, self-promoting agendas? Let's be quick to repent if we do.

We serve a righteous God who responds immediately to repentant hearts. As Psalm 51:17 says, "A broken and a contrite heart, O God, you will not despise."

In the end, it is not what we do for God that counts. It is why we do it. There is a great reward for those who serve Him with correct motives, for Jesus says, "Blessed are the pure in heart, for they will see God" (Matt. 5:8).

Many of us have been let down by someone who promised much but delivered little because the person's character did not match his or her statements. While it is true that faith is trust in God's word, we trust His word only because we have faith in its author and His integrity. Perhaps this is the most important aspect of faith. We know that God is dependable.

I have believed that for years, and many times have gone out on a limb to obey the Lord. But one day in 1985, a horrible tragedy severely tested me. God had never failed me, yet now I needed to take the biggest step of faith of my life while struggling through a major personal trauma.

CHAPTER NINE

Trusting God's Character

Following that eventful trip to India and Thailand, I was again preaching and teaching in Asia—and still trusting God for my finances.

I made it back to visit Baguio in early December, and Mike and Janice Shelling gave me a warm welcome. They had just fulfilled a one-year commitment in Manila and were happier than ever to be in Baguio. After years of preparation and waiting, they were about to move to the mountains north of the city to carry out their church planting vision.

Soon after I arrived, the Shellings invited me to their temporary house on Laubach Road. As I walked toward the house, my thoughts drifted to the many times our lives had intertwined over the years. And here we were together in Baguio again!

To get to their place, I walked past the house where Margaret and I had lived when we showed *Two a Penny*. The sight of our former brown wooden home and the yard where our two older children had played so happily triggered a flood of nostalgia. I felt so at home again, and I drank in the sights and memories until I found myself at the Shelling's front door. Janice welcomed me with her friendly greeting. In her arms was 3-month-old Jonathan, their latest arrival, and toddling nearby was energetic 2-year-old Melissa. Janice escorted me past a throng of other visitors into a bedroom where Mike sat propped up in bed.

Mike immediately apologized for an untimely illness. I was amazed that he was receiving other visitors in his house that afternoon. *Dear Mike. Even when he's not feeling well he's accommodating others and attending to their needs.*

As we talked alone in the bedroom, the main thing on his mind was his dream of moving further up into the mountains where he could live among the people and share the gospel with them.

"I've settled on a house to rent up there. We're just six weeks away from going!"

I could picture it in my mind. Mountain houses were not very big and usually met only basic needs. I felt very happy for this godly little family, who had been anticipating this day for years.

My visit to Baguio was over all too soon, and I was on the plane back to Hawaii thinking of the time my family and I would again be working in the Philippines. But for that to happen we needed to renew our long-term visas. Once in Kona, I decided to entrust our passports to a friend bound for Manila. Immigration officials would need our passports for a lengthy renewal process, and since I knew I wouldn't be traveling internationally for a while, it seemed like a good time to do it.

The next few weeks slipped by in a blur of activity. After the fun of the 1984 Christmas holidays, I resumed my independent study program at the University of the Nations, and Margaret continued her work in the university's administration office. In January, she also began playing the piano for a community musical production. The performances lasted a week, and after the final engagement on a Saturday night, we were planning to celebrate as soon as she returned home.

When darkness fell, I put Mark, Stuart, and Warren (now ages 12, 9, and 6) to bed in the loft of the large, open-air room on campus that we now called home. To help them get to sleep, I turned off all the lights except the reading lamp beside our bed downstairs. Very content with the restful peace, I quietly read.

It wasn't long before the ring of the telephone broke the silence.

I recognized the familiar voice of a friend on campus. She apologized that she had some bad news. My pulse quickened.

"Go ahead," I said, not knowing what to expect. I could feel my stomach tighten.

"We've just received a message from the YWAM center in Baguio." She paused for a slight moment. "Mike and Janice have been stabbed to death."

I stood in stunned silence as she spilled out the few details she had. The couple apparently had been robbed and murdered at night in that temporary Baguio home where I had visited them just a month earlier. The two children were safe. They had been found, many hours later, crying but physically unharmed.

Numb and distressed, I hung up the phone.

Dear Mike and Janice! A collage of memories flashed through my mind: the early days, our work and conversations together, and my efforts to encourage their relationship. *How could this happen in Baguio!* Margaret and I had lived there for ten peaceful years. Baguio, where we had enjoyed so much of life. The student center work, the movie showings, and the many outreaches we'd conducted. My mind refused to take in the traumatic news from that community to which we so belonged.

I had often left Margaret and the children in Baguio as I made trips throughout the country and beyond! We'd never been afraid of anything like this happening to us or our co-workers. If it had happened in any other city, I could have understood it. But not our beloved Baguio!

I suddenly felt afraid. My heightened emotions caused me to imagine that even the ordinary noises I heard in the next room were coming from somebody creeping up on me, knife in hand. *What is going on? What is happening to me?*

I fell to my knees and began to pray and sob. As I anguished over Mike and Janice, I wondered where Margaret was. She seemed a long time coming home. She finally came through the door, sweet and obviously happy. Tonight's performance must have gone exceptionally well.

"Is my one and only there?" she lovingly called from the door.

I looked up at her. The moment she saw me she knew something was terribly wrong. I choked up as I tried to give her the news, which only increased her anxiety. When I was able to tell her what had happened, she threw herself on the bed and wept. After a couple of agonizing minutes, the same spirit of fear that had gripped me suddenly seized her. She rose to her feet and locked the door. We lived in a peaceful community. We never locked our door at night. What was happening to us felt absurd!

For the next couple of days, I wept more than I can ever remember weeping before. My sister Elizabeth called the next day from New Zealand. She had known Mike from her time with us on the Asian Circle Team. I began sobbing all over again. Later I put through a call to Baguio. It took me a long time to stop weeping just to talk.

My thoughts turned to the idea of going to the Philippines, but I knew that wasn't possible. *What a time to be without my passport!* Someone suggested that I go to Minnesota for the memorial service to be held in Janice's hometown. That seemed logical. I knew Janice's parents and had once stayed on their farm for a couple of days. But in this emotional state, I did not trust myself to hear God clearly. I had learned the importance of not stepping out in any endeavor—particularly one necessitating the provision of finance—without a word from the Lord.

On Tuesday morning, two and a half days after hearing the news of the brutal double murder, I rose early to wait quietly before the Lord to hear what His will was. Should I go to Minnesota or not? My thoughts and expectation indicated I should. Near our room was the small office where I often prayed at this early hour. I got down on my knees, and leaning on a steel chair, I began to seek the Lord. When I reached the point in prayer where I felt I had died to what I thought or felt, I asked the question. I was not prepared for the answer.

You are not to go to Minnesota.

I jumped up, startled at what I had heard. Stretching my arms out wide in that tiny office, I cried out, "God, why ever not?"

Returning to my knees, I settled down to wait on the Lord. In a little while I heard Him gently speak again.

Because I want you to fly to the Philippines tonight and be at the actual funeral tomorrow.

I was simultaneously awestruck and bewildered.

"Lord," I said audibly, springing back onto my feet. "This is a big assignment. I need some confirmation about this!"

Monstrous obstacles were in my way. I had no passport, and I had never heard of anyone traveling intercontinentally without a passport unless he or she was a refugee. I also had no money. A round-trip fare to the Philippines from Hawaii was around $800, and I did not have a dollar towards that amount. This was nothing new, but I had to face it.

Another matter loomed in my mind. Only a nonstop flight on Philippine Airlines (PAL) would take me to Manila in time for the funeral in Baguio the next day. I was not even sure that such a flight departed that night.

Still, I knew that none of these obstacles would be insurmountable with the Lord.

"God, this is the biggest assignment I have ever received," I prayed as I held my Bible. "I ask You for confirmation. Please give me a verse that would help me to know that I really have heard from You."

Immediately, I sensed the words *Read Psalm 72:18* slip into my mind. I had no idea what that verse said. Curious, I flipped through the pages of my big black study Bible to the psalm. I was anxious for a second witness. My eyes settled on verse 18, which read: "Praise be to the Lord God, the God of Israel, who alone does marvelous deeds."

I stared at those words, aware that only marvelous deeds could get me to the Philippines. I was encouraged but cautious.

"Okay, Lord, I'll just take it one step at a time."

I knew that all my efforts wouldn't bring it to pass if it wasn't His will. Was there something I could do? I entered into a time of fierce spiritual warfare before returning to our room in time for breakfast with the family. Before I sat down at the table, something occurred to me. Only a PAL flight would get me to the Philippines in time for the funeral. If I were really up the creek, the huge airline book in the cupboard would tell me so. The schedule assured me that there was indeed a Philippine Airline flight tonight. So far I was on track.

My family had anticipated that I would travel to Minnesota. At breakfast, however, I gently announced what I felt I should do. Margaret was at first completely taken aback, but she rallied to be a great help.

Just one step at a time. That was all I could do and all that God required of me. Once the children had left for school and Margaret had gone off to her work at the office, I sat down with my Bible and began to pray. Since this assignment had been given to me with the shortest lead time ever, I really felt the need to press into God and commune with Him.

I hadn't been praying long when I was interrupted by the jingle of the phone. To my surprise, it was an agent for Aloha Airlines informing me that the company had heard of the tragedy and was offering me a round-trip ticket to Honolulu. *How encouraging of the Lord*, I thought, as I hung up the phone.

As I continued to pray and wait on God, Mr. Relova's name kept coming to mind. Mr. Relova was a vice-president of PAL who had helped me in various ways in Manila, but I'd heard that he now served Philippine Airlines in San Francisco. I wondered whether God wanted me to contact him for permission to take a flight without a passport. He seemed just the person to open the right doors. My mind also reviewed our Davao days when the former Air Manila manager had once obtained a "nonrevenue" ticket for me. I knew that such tickets existed, although they were generally reserved for government personnel or dire emergencies. I reasoned that perhaps they would consider the death of Mike and Janice to be such an emergency.

I pursued that thought in prayer. Should I contact Mr. Relova? Or would he be in London or Tokyo on one of his many trips abroad? Feeling a peace about contacting him, I put a call through to his direct line around 9 a.m.

The phone just rang and rang. Finally, a female Filipino voice explained that Mr. Relova would be out of his office for a few hours. I was disappointed that I'd not made immediate contact with my competent friend, but I left a message with the secretary regarding my request.

The call from San Francisco came in while I was eating lunch. In our past phone conversations, Mr. Relova had always greeted me as if I were a cherished brother. Today, however, his tone was uncharacteristically cool and businesslike.

"I have received your message," he began. "I am sorry, but I do not have the authority to grant your request. Our company can be fined $2,000 for carrying people without proper documentation."

My heart hit my shoes. I realized that he was not offering any alternative solution to my passport problem.

I could have ended the conversation there, hung up, and tried to forget the whole thing. After all, things were just not working out. But I also knew that the way of faith requires perseverance when God has given direction. Hadn't I seen God do enough impossible things for me to know that I couldn't just give up? Not without a fight, anyway.

A sudden thought popped into my mind, knowing that governments could override their airlines I politely inquired, "Can't the Philippine embassy help?"

For a moment there was silence at the other end.

"Well, what you could do is this. You could call one of your colleagues in Manila and ask him to pursue an *OK to board* permit from our downtown office in Manila."

Aha, so such a thing can be done!

A bit more encouraged, I decided to probe a little.

"Then how about a nonrevenue ticket?"

"Well...," he said with a hesitancy that told me he was not confident I could achieve my goal. "You could also ask your colleague to contact one of our other vice-presidents." He gave me a name and then added a word of encouragement before saying goodbye. "You still have time. It is only 6 a.m. in Manila."

Even so, I felt discouraged. I hadn't expected that the permission I was requesting would be routed through Manila. Time-consuming Filipino bureaucracy could take weeks!

Graeme, who I knew was living outside of Manila at the time, was the logical person to ask to do this legwork. But a special journey into Manila could take over four hours round-trip. It was the day before the funeral, and he and Mary had to make a five-and-a-half-hour trip themselves to get to the funeral in Baguio. Besides, Graeme had his own responsibilities. What if all this failed? Even though he was a close friend, it was a lot to ask of him.

I returned to the lunch table. June Coxhead, a YWAM staff writer and friend from New Zealand had joined us for lunch. I told Margaret and June the news.

"But I don't feel like making a quick decision to call Graeme," I said and slowly resumed eating my lunch. Margaret pondered my words and then hit me with a point that jolted me back to reality.

"Not to decide is to make a decision," she said succinctly. I knew exactly what she meant. It wasn't the first time that I'd marveled at how she could cut right to the heart of a matter. Usually she could say in one sentence what took me a paragraph. In this case, she meant that if I didn't make a decision, it was the same as deciding not to go to the Philippines.

"Let's pray, then," I replied, pushing my plate away from me. The question before us was whether I should ask Graeme at this busy time to handle the paperwork needed for my two special requests. We bowed our heads and prayed. I was impressed with the thought to call Graeme thirty minutes later. Margaret and June agreed that I should call.

Yet another challenge lay ahead. The phone where Graeme stayed was often out of order. I placed the call at the time God had specified. I heard the phone ringing, but I knew that it didn't mean a thing. The phone sounded like that even when it was not working! I tried to imagine what they were doing at 7 a.m. Suddenly I heard the receiver click. *The phone was working!*

Soon Graeme was on the line. We were both subdued, of course. Our friends' deaths were uppermost in our minds. After discussing the tragedy with Graeme, I approached him with the purpose of my call.

"I'd like to come across for the funeral. But there's a problem."

"You've got no money."

I smiled inwardly. Graeme knew exactly how I operated.

"And you guys have my passport," I added.

Since Graeme also knew of my relationship with Mr. Relova, I brought him up to date on our latest conversation. There was a pause at the other end.

"It would be good if you could come," he said warmly but thoughtfully. Then he made my heart leap.

"I'm just about to go downtown."

The timing of the call had been perfect, and I was thrilled that I wasn't asking Graeme to make a special four-hour round trip to Manila. But Graeme was a realist, and I knew that he was probably groaning inside with the thought of all the paperwork that a thing like this would entail in our adopted nation.

"Please don't feel that you have to knock yourself out on this," I stressed. "If this is of God, it'll come to pass."

"I can't spend all day on it, but I can start the process," he promised before we said our goodbyes. Good old Graeme! He was truly a faithful friend.

Neither of us would have been so cheerful, however, had we known how long and difficult the day would be. For me, the next four hours dragged by slowly. I passed the time gathering things for the trip and stuffing them into two small carry-on bags. I even went off for a while to my regular student work duty of mowing the grass. But nothing held my attention as I struggled with my strange travel plans. I found myself comparing them with the streamlined travel plans of others and wishing it were that easy for me. It wasn't long before I became discouraged again.

As the January afternoon shadows in Hawaii lengthened, I reached another hurdle. The 7:30 p.m. Aloha flight out of Kona was the last flight I could take on my free ticket, even though the PAL flight did not take off from Honolulu until 3 a.m. If I were going, I'd need to get to the Kona airport within the next two hours. But then, I hadn't heard a word from anyone about the progress on my two requests.

Just before 5 p.m., I placed a call to the manager of Philippine Airlines in Honolulu explaining my contact with Mr. Relova in San Francisco and Graeme in Manila. Had he heard anything? He hadn't. But about 30 minutes later he called back.

"I'm sorry, but I cannot allow you on board tonight. I have just called Manila and they haven't even heard of you!"

I did some quick calculations. It was only 11:30 a.m. in the Philippines. It would have taken Graeme two hours to get down-town, and he probably had things to do on the way. I tried pointing this out, but the manager remained pessimistic. Later I was to learn that he had been told not to allow me on board under any circumstances.

I slowly hung up the phone and brought Margaret up to date.

"So what will you do now?" she asked.

I didn't know, but I wasn't ready to give up completely. "All I need is some small miracle, some sign to get me going again."

I have found in this faith walk that God is prepared to provide encouragements on the way. In the Bible, He inspired Gideon when his faith was down. I needed to know I was still on the right track. On this occasion I didn't have long to wait. The phone rang again a few minutes later.

"Hello, this is the Philippines calling."

I immediately recognized the familiar sound of a Filipino long-distance operator. Soon a PAL official from Manila was on the line, excitedly speaking in his accented English.

"Mr. Tooley, Mr. Tooley, are you there? I have here your permit to board our flight tonight! But I have been unable to contact our Honolulu manager. Earlier I told him not to board you! But it is okay now. You can just tell him!"

His excitement was contagious.

Remembering the station manager's pessimism just five minutes earlier, I eagerly countered, "Please send him a telex. He might not believe me!"

I then asked about the nonrevenue ticket.

"Oh, I don't know anything about that," he replied. "Another department would have to approve that request. But your friend Mr. Jones is standing here. Would you like to speak to him?"

Graeme was in high spirits. He hadn't expected to be this far along in the paperwork, but he was encouraged by how easy this part of the bureaucratic trip had been.

I hurriedly finished packing my carry-on bags, said a quick goodbye to my family, and headed for the airport. I had just enough time to catch the last flight to Honolulu. My flight, however, was delayed an hour, which I found difficult to accept. I would much rather have spent the time at home, sorting out a disagreement between one of my sons and another child that had resulted in harsh words and tears just ten minutes before I left. Now I had an hour to waste instead of getting to the root of these children's problem. The faith walk is never easy. It seems the timing of such problems can be inspired by the devil himself. But it reinforced what I had learned elsewhere: I need to keep spiritually alert during these special adventures. Finding a pay phone, I called my family.

Once in Honolulu, I approached a young Filipina at the Philippine Airlines check-in area. I explained my circumstances and asked whether she had a message for me.

"I haven't received anything," she replied. "But could you just wait for a moment?" she asked politely and then disappeared, leaving me at the counter, where I prayed. She returned a few minutes later reading a telex.

"Here it is," she said, "You're cleared to board without your passport."

"Great! Is there anything on there about a nonrevenue ticket?" I queried.

"No, I'm sorry. There is nothing."

"Oh well," I replied, "there is still time. The flight doesn't leave for another six hours, and in Manila it's only 3 p.m. Could you book me a window seat please?"

Six hours to wait. I peeked into my wallet. I had exactly three dollars. But there was something reassuring about that amount. On both trips to India last year, it was extraordinary how often I would arrive at a foreign airport and all I had to turn into local currency was $3. I was once again down to that familiar amount. *Well, I guess I can buy a cup of coffee in the cafeteria and spend a couple hours writing letters while I wait.*

I began writing, but I looked at my watch frequently to calculate what time it would be in Manila. I prayed often. Had I known what Graeme was facing on my behalf, I would have prayed harder.

Around 11 p.m., I left the cafeteria to check with the PAL office again. Nothing more had come in. I told myself it was only 5 p.m. in the Philippines and the office approving my passage would be open for another two hours. There was still time. But it was a nerve-racking experience nonetheless.

While standing at the PAL desk, I watched nearby passengers

slowly move towards the Pan Am counter. Suddenly I stood up straighter. Wasn't that Bob, my pastor back in New Zealand many years ago? He had been on the original New Zealand YWAM board I'd set up in 1969. I hadn't seen him in ten years.

"What are you doing at Honolulu airport in the middle of the night?" he exclaimed.

Our initial shouts of surprise quickly turned to sober conversation when I broke the news about Mike. Bob and his wife, Noelle, knew the Shelling family, who had lived in New Zealand since their shift from Australia.

"I'm trying to get on a flight to the Philippines," I explained.

He thought I was merely trying to get on a booked-up flight, and I was happy to let him think that. It can sometimes be embarrassing to explain my adventures in faith, especially when they are of this magnitude.

"After you get your boarding pass," he invited, "come and see us at Gate 19 for some fellowship." I agreed to.

Eleven-thirty came and went. So did midnight and twelve-thirty. There was no further news. At twelve-fifty, feelings of despair and near bitterness began to rise within me. I fought the attack, rebuking the devil in Jesus' name while I marched to the Philippine Airlines counter. *I am not going to feel this way!*

As I reached the desk, a Filipina waving a piece of paper called out to me.

"Mr. Tooley, Mr. Tooley, we've been paging you. Here it is! Your passage round-trip all the way to Baguio!" She seemed to be even more excited than I was.

"You're booked to Manila, but unfortunately you're only on the waiting list for the flight to Baguio."

God, you've done it again!

Relieved to be embarking on the next segment of the trip, I waited as she processed my boarding pass for the window seat. I knew I wasn't out of the woods yet. I still had to get on that flight to Baguio if I were to make it in time for the funeral. But if God could bring me this far, he surely could get me to Baguio on time.

The Filipina handed me the ticket wallet and wished me well. Her cheerful and gracious attitude made me feel I was already back in the Philippines!

It was a long walk to Gate 19 to say goodbye to Bob and Noelle, but I didn't mind. I had a lot to meditate on. I'd been up for twenty-one hours seeing God at work, and my heart was light. I now had only a dollar note and some loose change in my pocket, but I didn't care. I had to stir Bob and Noelle from their slumber.

"You're looking at a miracle!" I said, thrusting the prized ticket toward my drowsy friends. When I'd finished telling my story, Bob reached into his pocket.

"Noelle and I have talked about this, and we'd like to give you these," he said, peeling off three twenty-dollar bills. I'd not mentioned my own personal needs, but God knew and had provided in another remarkable way. We talked nonstop until their flight was called and they headed towards their Pan Am clipper jet.

I made my way back to the PAL boarding area. For the first time, I took a moment to examine my ticket and discovered it wasn't a ticket at all but rather was a pass![1] For the duration of the coming flights, PAL was treating me as an honorary employee, and I had the privilege of traveling standby status. Fortunately, the flight tonight was not full.

It was 3 a.m. when I walked through the jetway towards the entrance of the Boeing 747 aircraft. I couldn't help but stop and linger at the doorway for a moment and be in awe of an incredible God.

"I'm getting on this flight, Lord, as you directed," I prayed silently. "Even though I have neither a passport nor a ticket, you have opened the way for me!"

I continued on and found my seat by the window. The woman sitting beside me was a Christian who had heard of the Shelling murders. She handed me a Philippine tabloid with the story of the tragedy on the front page. The sensational way in which the story was written revolted me. I relived the horror of the senseless acts of violence and yet again felt fear rise within me.

[1.] I learned from Graeme later that the practice of PAL issuing special passes had been discontinued prior to my request, which made this provision even more exceptional. Since then, the leadership of PAL has passed to others, who today would frown on such a request.

Weary as I was, I didn't sleep much during that nine-hour flight. Sitting in the dark, I was constantly reminded of the murders and of the fact that I was traveling to the scene of a brutal crime.

When the sun finally rose, my spirits rose with it. Soon the hazy skyline of Manila appeared in the distance, and I sat staring out toward Manila Bay with my seat belt fastened for landing. My seat mate's friendly voice finally interrupted my somber thoughts.

"I would like you to take this," she said, handing me a ten-dollar bill. I thanked her and inwardly shook my head in wonder. I had seen God provide in dozens of ways over the years, but this was the first time it had happened in flight!

It was early morning Philippine time when we arrived at Manila's international airport. At 7:15 a.m. I learned that I was number six on the waiting list for the only flight of the day to Baguio, scheduled to leave in three hours. I considered taking a bus to Baguio, but that would take at least six hours, putting me there well after the funeral.

A new struggle surfaced. I reasoned that if I couldn't get on this flight, I'd have to take the bus anyway. Why not just get the bus in the first place? But God had said I should be at the funeral, so I finally stuck with my original plan. And sure enough, I was rewarded with a seat. As I walked out on the tarmac to board the plane, I cast a wary look at the gray skies overhead. It was not a good sign. I knew Baguio's airport at 5,000 feet had no radar facilities, and planes could not land in heavy overcast conditions. On numerous occasions, a plane I was booked on had been denied landing for this very reason.

My heart began to sink again as the turboprop climbed through darkening skies. After all this effort, it would be a pity if we had to land at San Fernando, La Union, an hour and a half away from Baguio by road. I'd miss the funeral. Suddenly the plane flew into brilliant sunshine, and we touched down right on schedule at 11:05 a.m. I was already five minutes late for the funeral and faced a 15-minute ride into town.

Tightening my grip on my two hand-carried bags, I strode through the tiny arrival area and hailed the first taxi I saw. I told the driver to go as fast as he could. He took me literally and gunned the engine of his rattly old taxi down the bumpy roads at a reckless speed. But we did make good time. As we stopped outside the Lutheran church, I could hear a hymn.

I paid the taxi driver with money Bob had given me at the Honolulu airport, grabbed my luggage, and entered the church packed out with mountain people in honor of Mike and Janice. Once inside, I realized I had missed very little of the service.

Here I was. I had arrived as the Lord had instructed me the day before. "Praise be to the Lord God,..., who alone does marvelous deeds" (Psalm 72:18).

Trusting God's Character

In many ways we have come full circle on our discussion about faith. In an early chapter we talked about unbelief being a lack of trust in God's loving character. When we operate in faith, we see that God is totally dependable; that is, where He guides He provides. I believe we cannot walk in faith and be fatalistic at the same time. We must actively press in to hear His voice and obey His promptings. We need to exercise a faith that says, "I'm doing what you told me to do, God. I believe You will provide, and I know You love me. I totally believe in Your character!"

To cope with such situations as the Shellings' deaths, we must have unswerving faith in God's character. God is righteous and never does anything wrong. Perhaps the following is a partial answer to the question, Why does God let good people die?

If Christianity could promise that no one would ever fall sick, suffer a tragedy, or be killed, millions would embrace it. But Christianity cannot do that. To embrace Christ for selfish reasons goes against God's character. God is love, and He is seeking people who will embrace Him out of a heart of pure love and obedience. Job knew that well, for he said, "Though he slay me, yet will I trust in him" (Job 13:15, KJV).

We will have to wait until we get to heaven to find out all the reasons for the tragedies we've encountered. As for the Shellings, it was a great comfort for me to learn that in their will, they had provided for Melissa and Jonathan to be placed in the care of Janice's brother and his wife, Loren and Darlene Synstilien. At the time of the Shellings' deaths, the couple in Minnesota had been exploring the possibility of adopting two children—a boy and a girl.

The episode serves to recap many of the principles of faith already mentioned. First, it underscores the importance of hearing from God and receiving confirmation of His guidance. I was not willing to make the long and involved trip to the funeral without first having God confirm the earlier impression. His confirmation came when the Holy Spirit gave me the chapter and verse of an encouraging psalm, although it could have come through a variety of other means.

For confirmation to be of God, it must bring peace to our hearts. In fact, peace in our hearts can *be* sufficient confirmation in itself. Writing in the sky without our having peace within is not guidance, for the Bible says peace is to be our guide (Col. 3:15).

Also, for every major trip I make, Margaret has to be in agreement, or I stay home. It would be unfair to her to have to take sole responsibility for the family if she had no authority to confirm or not confirm the trip in the first place.

Another principle that emerges from this chapter is that God wants to encourage us when we are in the midst of very difficult circumstances. In the book of Judges, the Lord told Gideon to slay the Amelekites. Yet God found it necessary to say to Gideon one day, "If you are afraid to attack, go down to the camp...and listen to what they are saying. Afterward, you will be encouraged to attack...." (Judges 7:10-11).

The fact that Gideon crept up to the enemy camp proves he was in need of encouragement. He took heart when he overheard the Amelekites prophesying their own doom at Gideon's hand.

When the Honolulu PAL manager explained that he'd been told to deny my boarding, I needed reassurance. Once I received that surprise call from the excited Philippine Airlines official in Manila, I was ready to again rocket forward.

The reassurance is not often circumstantial with me however. Usually it comes through God giving me the witness of His Holy Spirit that I really am on the right track. Reassurance may also come through a verse of Scripture leaping off the page during my daily Bible reading.

God is an encourager. Tap into that aspect of His character!

The events of this chapter also illustrate the need for perseverance and for keeping spiritually alert. To me the emotional attack I experienced at the Honolulu airport was satanic vindictiveness. Once he knew he couldn't stop what God had set in motion, Satan wanted to afflict me with a severe emotional onslaught in the hope I would get bitter at God. I'm glad I didn't give in. Had I yielded, I would have been robbed of the joy at the point of victory later on.

Recognizing the attacks of the enemy, and then resisting them, is part of spiritual warfare. I now recognize that the fear that came upon me when I heard about the murders was a spiritual attack. Years later I was in real danger in a certain area of the world where Westerners are often kidnapped. God had spoken to me to make the trip, and He protected me, despite a rumor that the building where I stayed one night had been targeted by local terrorists. Later I learned that I had been followed by the kidnappers. Although I was on a dangerous mission, I was not hampered by fear.

Another question that obviously presents itself is, Why did God want me to be at that funeral anyway? As I have witnessed for Christ, I have sometimes retold this story to illustrate that Christianity means knowing and walking with God. Christianity is not just a religion of rituals and dead dogmas. Whenever I tell this story, or similar stories, non-Christians see my point and become more receptive to the gospel.

The best answer as to why God took me to the funeral is this: The Philippines had been our adopted country for thirteen years. The Filipino staff members regarded Margaret and me as the older brother and sister of their new family. Many of them had suffered rejection from their own families for obeying God and becoming missionaries.

In that time of great grief caused by the brutal murders, God was honoring the family orientation so valued by Filipinos. He also honored my desire to be with my adopted countrymen. I needed their love and fellowship at this time of deep sorrow, and they needed mine. God plucked me off an obscure island in the middle of the Pacific and flew me through the night without a passport or a ticket to honor the bond of love, trust, and fellowship that existed among us.

I am so grateful He did!

Afterwords

Although I have other faith stories that I have not told in this book, those recorded here represent the teachings I feel God would have me share at this time. The stories not in the book often follow a familiar script: *receive a word from God, begin to follow God's leading, encounter opposition, wage spiritual warfare, and then experience the fulfillment of what God said.*

One example is the time I felt God guide me to write something for a Baguio newspaper. With article in hand, I excitedly approached the editor with two requests: Would he publish it, and could I write a column every week?

Although both proposals were rejected, I eventually did write weekly, and those writings were regularly the focus of classroom discussions at a Baguio college. The editor became a friend who later helped our *Two a Penny* and other showings.

The incidents of hearing God's voice are the features of most of my stories. This practice is essential to faith. It is vital. As I pointed out in the introduction to the book, we must receive some go-ahead from God before we step out in faith. Most Christians would obey Him if they could just be sure it was really God who was speaking to them. I encourage everyone to develop this ability, since without it, it is impossible to perform exploits in faith.

Some have suggested that the adventures I describe in the book happened to me because I have the "gift of faith" as mentioned in 1 Cor. 12:9. I have usually linked the gift of faith to the healing ministry, although I'm sure it is not restricted to that. If I do have the gift of faith, it must seldom come upon me, as often I have to really work at doing what God has laid on my heart to do.

Some may ask why there has been no mention of healings in this book. While I have learned lessons while praying in faith for the sick, my stories are too short to fill out a chapter. One thing I've learned is that it helps me if I receive a quickening in my spirit that something is really going to happen. This occurred when Paul saw that the lame man "had faith to be healed" (Acts 14:8-10). But it doesn't happen all the time. Most times, I pray for the sick on the basis of God's loving character, and people have been healed that way. But why some are healed and many are not is a question I feel unqualified to answer.

I do believe that more healings occur when we have genuine compassion for the afflicted. That is a vital key exemplified by Jesus when He was on earth. Another is to not give up easily. The Scriptures encourage us to persist in prayer without giving in to discouragement (Luke 11:5-13; 18:1-7).

Another key that has worked for me is to be part of a group while praying for the sick. Some outstanding miracles of healing have occurred this way, but interestingly, not in the same way as when I have prayed alone. Praying for the sick seems to be such a complex issue. I am happy to pray for the sick and am grateful for the times people are healed.

Our Film Ministry

We have many more stories about our adventures showing films, including the time we took 16mm films along the mountain trail in the Cordilleras north of Baguio and showed them wherever we could find a generator. Because in those days a movie was a rarity, crowds of sometimes 1,000 would stand to watch the entire film.

We even hired the Quirino Cinema in Baguio in 1978 and ran Christian films twelve hours a day for two months. The adventure had both its high and its low spots. One difficulty was finding enough Christian films to screen during the second month.

Another problem was that we couldn't expect high schools and colleges to assign their students to watch our movies week after week. But the two-month experience was worth it. Thousands heard the Word of God through this venture in faith.

In past generations, oratory and the printed page were the most influential forces around. That has changed. The world is now powerfully affected by every blockbuster movie that hits the big screen. These movies are dubbed into a multitude of foreign languages and then watched in theaters by millions around the world. But it doesn't stop there. Later they are run and rerun on the world's television networks and are made available in video stores, which are springing up like mushrooms all over the globe. Add to this the reviews in newspapers and magazines with large circulations and we see something of the extent to which these films further influence our world.

And don't forget that perhaps an even more persuasive influence is the amount of time these movies are discussed among family, friends, and co-workers as well as in a variety of other social settings. These movies are changing the way society thinks and therefore how it acts; what it considers to be right and wrong; and how people perceive God, themselves, and their fellow man.

Christians must not abdicate this market. We need to get in there with our message. A blockbuster movie about the book of Acts could wipe out a lot of people's resistance to the gospel. I would also love to see a movie based on the book *Pontius Pilate* by Paul L. Maier. Scenes of Pilate summoning both Jewish and Roman officials to locate Jesus' body would convince many about the validity of the resurrection.

The decision to show today the movies we used twenty years ago would depend entirely on the leading of the Lord. If we really hear from God on the choice of a movie—especially in a developing country—and the screening is bathed in prayer, we can expect wonderful results, not only through the message of the film but also through the contacts made while promoting the film. With *The Hiding Place*, for example, most of the evangelism related to its showing took place in the schools and civic clubs and over the air.

It must be remembered that in the 1970s the Philippines was considered the third largest English-speaking country in the world.

I would still use English movies there today, but I would be more interested in screening those in the local dialects more suited to the culture. While we lived in the Philippines, Christ for Greater Manila produced a movie called *Teresa* in the Tagalog dialect. It attracted large crowds whenever we showed it on streets or in basketball courts, and it always gave us the valuable opportunity to preach afterward (or during the changing of the reels).

Whether showing older or current Christian films, it is important to get into film and video in any way you can, since these media influence how people currently think and act.

Finances

I am now 49 years of age and have lived without a salary for twenty-nine years. I still do not possess a credit card, and I have lost count of the number of countries where I ran out of money. Many times, as you know, I didn't even have an airline ticket to travel to the next country. Despite this, God's provision has been real. In twenty-nine years, I can remember only three times missing a meal because I didn't have the money. When I recently mentioned this to Margaret, she thought for a moment and then replied that she couldn't remember missing even one meal for lack of money. Our four children can confirm this.

This is not to say that as a family we haven't skimped at times. Often we have had to be content with what we had, such as clothing or furniture, until extra money came in. Years ago, Margaret and I sometimes wrote letters and then had to wait for money for postage before we could mail them. We also went through lean times when the bills piled up. But the work we did for God never ceased. That's the important thing, as is God's faithfulness.

Some may wonder if my policy of not asking for money still continues.

Today we do not advertise our needs very often, but from time to time we do ask for help. Occasionally, we will explain how funds can be sent so that a donor can receive a tax-deductible receipt. At times we will mention a specific need, such as traveling as a family.

In the past twelve years, I have approached about ten people or churches to support us monthly. A number of them have responded and helped us for a while. Three continue to help. In contrast to that, other people have voluntarily supported us uninterrupted for over ten years or more!

I hope this book will reach many full-time Christian workers from developing nations who have few people to turn to for financial help. I want them to know that God is concerned about them regardless of their location. In the Philippines as a 20-year-old with few contacts but with trust in a loving God, I saw Him supply under improbable circumstances. Twice I went to catch an interprovincial bus with insufficient money for the fare. On both occasions, God moved someone to thrust money into my hand just before I reached the road. Neither person knew that I was in need.

I have never been left at the airport without a ticket. However, I did try twice to take Margaret with me, but neither attempt turned out well. Each time I felt uneasy about both of us going, but regretfully I ignored those God-given nudges. On one occasion, Margaret simply didn't go, and on the other, her ticket (bought on an invoice) didn't get paid for immediately after we returned from the trip, which embarrassed me greatly.

I speak constantly to missionary candidates giving testimony to God's faithful provision. For years I have usually been able to say that I have no debts beyond current bills. Mind you, we have very few assets. Just six months ago, we bought our very first car. Before that, we had been given five cars outright and offered the use of several others, including a couple of very good cars. In 1988, for example, we were given a 1984 top-of-the-line Ford Tempo GLX with only 35,000 miles on the odometer. Incidentally, we had more trouble with the car we bought than with any of our gift cars!

Although I don't have a credit card, there have been a few times that I have borrowed money, but they were the exception rather than the rule. For example, I used the overdraft facility on our bank account twice for air tickets. The last time I deliberately used an overdraft facility was in 1974. Borrowing is not a way of life for us.

At this point, I have not made any provision for my retirement years. I am not against God telling me to do something regarding retirement, but that hasn't happened yet. Recently, I was struck by Jesus' comment that birds do not "store away in barns, and yet your heavenly Father feeds them" (Matt. 6:26). I am encouraged that we humans are more valuable than birds. A subsequent verse implies that God will supply for those humans who have not stored things away in barns but have been busy building the Kingdom of God more than anything else (Matt. 6:33).

In 1991, God in His perfect timing directed us to take a sabbatical. Unknown to us, Margaret and I both had low-grade bacterial infections that had escaped detection for years. At that time I was extremely tired, having led six YWAM schools plus their outreaches virtually back to back. After twenty-two years of living outside our homeland, we were eager for a long rest, free from hectic ministry in the public eye. We could have said, "Who will look after us financially?" But we didn't, because we knew God would do that. And He did.

Although we found the country in the depths of a recession, God was a step ahead of us. Before we had even arrived, we received the biggest cash gift of our lives. For over a year, we were also given a rent-free cottage on three acres of prime land in one of Auckland's fashionable suburbs. And if that weren't enough, my brother Dale, then in business, lent us a Honda station wagon, which he later gave us outright, with the understanding that we would sell it at the end of our stay and put the money into our return airfares, which we did.

This time of healing and refreshment spoke to me about real retirement one day. God is not going to say, "Well, I looked after you all those years as you worked for Me, but now that you have retired, you are on your own!"

We do not as yet own a house, although I am certainly not against that. But we have lived in so many countries that it would be difficult to have to sell and buy a house each time we moved, even if we had the money. Recently, the apartment we rent was up for sale, and we were faced with the unhappy prospect of moving out. But then some dear friends heard about our situation. They had future family reasons for buying the apartment, but their immediate interest was to help us stay put. We truly can testify that God looks after our housing needs.

In 1994, we were faced with the decision regarding which

Hawaii high school one of our sons should attend. Because of our son's special situation and his particular needs, I concluded that the only righteous choice was the most expensive one. But the cost of $3,500 a year was completely out of our financial range. Margaret and I made the choice anyway. When an aunt died soon after that, I inherited some money for the first time in my life. The amount when converted into U.S. money at the current rate of exchange was approximately $3,500!

During that year, we began to wonder how we would manage the following year. But God again supplied, this time through very different channels. He continues to honor our decision, which we based on what God would want for our child, not on what would be the least expensive.

After all these years of trusting God for finances and seeing God supply so faithfully, I believe that there are two vital keys to God's provision. There is a proverb that says that if you give a man a fish he'll have food for that day. But if you give him a fish hook, he'll have food for the rest of his life!

I believe that the "hook" of that proverb signifies the importance of these two keys: the first is that we must live within our means and therefore say no to things we can't afford. In the West we often simply cannot bear to be without. As a result, we sometimes fail to distinguish between needs and wants and resort to the speedy use of a credit card. But our efforts at instant gratification are a means of dodging discipline and even avoiding what God is trying to tell us.

Doing without for a while has its benefits, although I am not preaching poverty. The apostle Paul didn't teach it, for he knew what it was to be in need *and* to have plenty (Phil. 4:12). To be always without finances is not healthy, but to always have plenty can actually make a person spiritually lethargic. Scripture warns "when you eat and are satisfied, be careful that you do not forget the Lord" (Deut. 6:11-12).

The second key is Jesus' admonition in Matt. 6:33. If we worry about the Kingdom of God and with forming godly character, God will concern Himself with regards to our money. He won't carry that burden, however, if our priority is to watch every latest movie, wear the most modern fashions, or eat at gourmet restaurants.

Over the years, God has supplied not only for us as a family but also for YWAM bases and schools that we have led. Amazing gifts have appeared from very unexpected sources for our operations as we have made our priority a concern for the state of His Kingdom. I think the real key is: Do we have a love for the lost, or are we just interested in surviving financially?

When we get to heaven, God is not going to ask us how much money we made, how big our house was, or how many cars we had in the garage. He will just want to know how much we loved Him and the sinful world He died for.

Epilog

Ten years have passed since the drama of Chapter 9, and we are still based in Kona. Margaret is the campus librarian, and I am involved in a variety of activities, mainly teaching, traveling, and writing. Since 1987 I have led five YWAM mission schools and taken the students to Asia. A number of incidents from these trips have found their way as anecdotes into the 1993 edition of my book *We Cannot But Tell,* a book on personal evangelism. I look forward to leading another missions school in 1996.

Our son Mark made several evangelism tours to Europe during his late teens and is now pursuing an engineering degree in New Zealand. Stuart is also in New Zealand and works in a bank. Warren and our fourth boy, Hudson, are with us and attend school in Kona.

Graeme and Mary Jones and their three children are on sabbatical in New Zealand after having spent more than twenty years in the Philippines. Before they left, they were supervising five YWAM operating locations in the Mindanao region from their home in Davao. They await God's direction for their future in missions.

After being adopted by their uncle and aunt in Minnesota, Melissa and Jonathan Shelling have enjoyed the warm love of eight other sets of aunts and uncles. Melissa, now twelve, told me recently she has no conscious memory of the ordeal that took the lives of their birth parents. A memorial fund has been set up in Mike's name at the University of the Nations, Kona campus, for the benefit of Filipino students to do post-Discipleship Training School studies.

Rey Yap is now an advertising consultant but also preaches and makes Christian videos, while Jack is now the academic dean of a Bible college in the Philippines. Helen and her husband Juan travel throughout the Philippines teaching on prayer and intercession. Recently, their ministry took them to India.

Kel Steiner took over leadership of YWAM Philippines when Margaret and I left. He now resides in New Zealand with his wife Kristyn and three children. Kel is the Dean of Missions at Faith Bible College, where I first met him while recruiting for the Asian Circle Team, and is making an invaluable contribution to the school.

On a trip to the Philippines in 1995, I enjoyed a long visit with Mrs. Teh, who was as hospitable as always, feeding me Chinese delicacies. I read her the contents of Chapter 7 and asked her permission to include those events in this book just as they happened. She readily agreed.

"If it will help people, Ross, please do."

Mrs. Teh has shut down her kung fu and other non-Christian movie business. She now maintains an office in a large distributing firm in Manila called Praise Inc., where she distributes Christian films, videos, and music.

And YWAM in the Philippines? After we left in 1983, the work increased dramatically under the leadership of Kel Steiner and Larry Baldock. The headquarters moved to Manila, where our outreach teams had worked for years. There are five branches in the Mindanao region, three in the Visayas, and many throughout Luzon, including Baguio and the mountain region north of the city.

It will soon be twenty-five years since the beginning of continuous YWAM ministry in the Philippines. The current staff of 200 plan to hold twenty-fifth anniversary celebrations over several weeks in mid-1997. In faith, I look forward to joining them in celebration!

Reading List

Books about Rees Howell, Hudson Taylor, and George Müller inspired me as a teenager. Remarkably, biographies of these men are still in print, although they come in various versions. If you can't get a copy from a Christian bookseller, you can find these books (or similar books) in numerous church libraries.

- *Rees Howell Intercessor*, by Norman Grubb. Christian Literature Crusade.
- *George Müller, Man of Faith and Miracles*, by Basil Miller. Bethany House.
- *Hudson Taylor and Maria, Pioneers in China*, by John Pollock. Zondervan.